Much of the original character art in this book was created by Nicholas Wan, and further developed by Garret Gioia.

Thank you to Scratch for their open license to use screenshots of the Scratch Editor, as well as image assets from their support materials library. Scratch is developed by the Lifelong Kindergarten Group at the MIT Media Lab. See http://scratch.mit.edu.

Codecampus, LLC
1691 Kettering
Irvine, CA 92614

www.codecampus.com

support@codecampus.com

About the Author

Hi! My name is Raj Sidhu.

I've been programming for nearly a decade, both for myself and for a variety of tech companies. In 2014 I founded codeCampus - an organization that has now taught over 2,000 teachers and 100,000 children (and counting) how to code. codeCampus has helped school districts all over the United States develop computer science enrichment curricula and opportunities for their students, and has consulted for companies including Nickelodeon and Dreamworks.

My firm belief is that computer science is a skill that can be learned and used by absolutely anyone - regardless of their gender, wealth, or hometown. And my goal is to help as many children as possible recognize coding for what it is: a medium for creativity, color, and progress.

Author's Note

It's easy to feel like technology is magic. I mean, who could ever understand how a smartphone works? Or what the Internet is? Or how these things were built, or where they came from? Aren't these answers just for super geniuses or something?

Believe it or not, every app, game, or website that you've ever used started as a human being's idea. That person used their imagination, determination, and **code** to pull that idea out of their minds and onto devices like computers, phones, or tablets for people all over the world to use and enjoy. And most of them aren't super geniuses - they're just people like you and me.

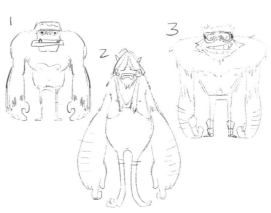

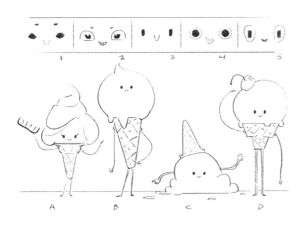

Technology itself isn't magic. But learning to *create technology* is real magic. It gives you (yes, **you**!) the incredible power to create things that can make people's lives better, or more fun, or more beautiful. The best part? Anyone can learn. Especially you.

This book will help you to understand how a lot of the technology we take for granted actually works, and teach you how to create magic of your own. It was a joy to write, and I hope you enjoy reading it, too.

- Raj

Heya, coders! My name is Synthia. I'm your friendly, neighborhood Artificial Intelligence, and for the rest of this book I'm going to be your guide through the wonderful world of coding. It's nice to e-meet you!

My friends and I love to code. Let me introduce you to the rest of the crew.

GAMEBOT

Even though it only knows 26 words, Gamebot's the life of the party. It's always down to let someone play a game, and tells the funniest jokes.

Gamebot was originally just a normal arcade machine. But then Wizard wrote a few extra lines of code for it, and it came to life!

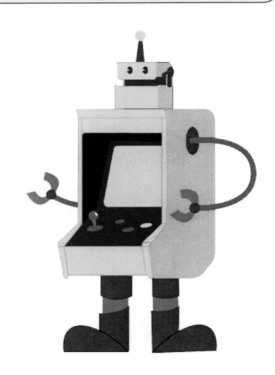

Wizard

Fun fact #1: Wizard used to be evil. Yeah, he had a big spooky tower and turned princes into animals and stuff. But then he started learning how to code, made friends with the rest of the gang, and turned out okay!

Fun fact #2: Wizard is 972 years old. Don't tell him I told you.

Tenta

Everybody in the group knows that Tenta's the best coder, and also the 2nd best baker behind Yeti.

She's been coding for about 5 years, and after college she plans on starting her own tech company.

Yeti

Yeti grew up on the slopes of the Alps teaching snowmen how to snowboard. He eventually decided to learn how to code to make his dreams of becoming a game developer come true.

Yeti's the biggest, and likes to pretend that he's the meanest, but really he's just the biggest sweetheart of the group.

Scoop

The group adopted Scoop after an outing to the local ice cream parlor a few years back. Gamebot looked down at his ice cream cone, saw that it was looking back at him, and that was that! They took him home, named him Scoop, and taught him how to code.

Chapter 1
What is code?

What is Code?

Code is step-by-step instructions that humans write to teach computers to do "stuff". The computer reads the instructions (code) written by the human, and follows them step-by-step until the computer is finished. The "stuff" that the human wanted to happen happens, and everyone is happy!

See, computers are extremely powerful machines. But they basically don't know how to do anything on their own.

That's why they need humans like us to teach them how to do stuff!

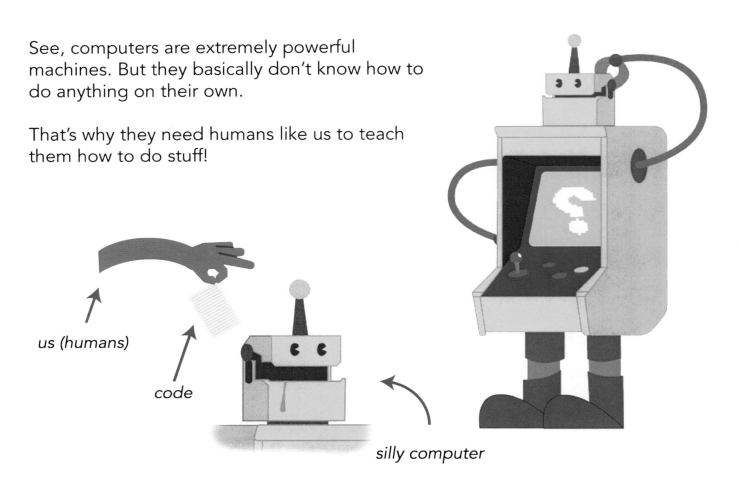

us (humans)

code

silly computer

How does it work? Well, first, we start with **an idea** for what we want our computer to do.

Next, we need to think about how to **turn that idea into step-by-step instructions**.

Finally, **we need a way to give those instructions to the computer**.

For example, let's say that we have an idea for an animation. In this animation, we want a cat to say hello, and then fly from the left side of the screen to the right side.

If we wanted to write our step-by-step instructions (code) for this idea in plain English, it might look something like this:

| 1. Start at the left side of the screen |
| 2. Say, "Hello" |
| 3. Glide to the right side of the screen |
| 4. Stop the animation |

Let's consider a few things about the way these instructions are written:

- The instructions are written ONE AT A TIME, top to bottom, left to right.

- Only one thing happens in each step

- If you changed the order of these steps, the whole animation would change

Whenever we write code, we'll need to keep these 3 points in mind!

Sandwiches & Sequence

Think about coding like making a peanut butter & jelly sandwich. When we (or our parents) make a PB&J, we need to follow a set of instructions in a very specific order. Otherwise, our sandwich will turn out all wrong!

PB&J Instructions!

1.) Walk to the fridge
2.) Open the fridge
3.) Pickup the peanut butter
4.) Pickup the jelly
5.) Pickup the bread
6.) Close the fridge
7.) Walk to the counter
8.) Place the ingredients on the counter
9.) Walk to the drawer
10.) Open the drawer
11.) Pickup a knife
12.) Close the drawer
13.) Walk to the counter
14.) Unscrew the peanut butter jar lid
15.) Take out a piece of bread
16.) Spread the peanut butter on the bread
17.) . . .

For example, look very carefully at the instructions to the left. See how each step **must** be done in the order it was written? What do you think would happen if we switched steps 1 and 2? What about steps 7 and 8?

Do I...dip the bread?

If we don't write our code carefully, making sure that we have every step we need and that each step is in its proper place, then our computers will get very confused.

This is called **sequence** - the order that code is written in!

What can we make with code?

We now know that code is just a way for humans to write instructions for computers, so that those computers can perform tasks. But what kind of tasks can computers be taught to do?

Animations

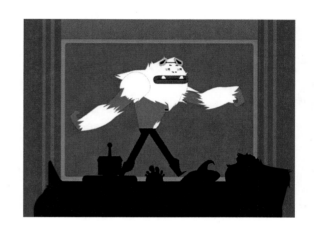

Animations - like the ones you see in cartoons, or in video games - are made up of thousands of still pictures that are played one after another to make it look like the still images are actually a fluid video. This can be a very difficult process, so professional animators use code to simplify their jobs!

Applications (apps)

Have you ever used a digital calculator, or checked the weather on a phone or computer? Have you ever taken a photo with a digital camera, or used a web browser like Google Chrome?

These are all examples of apps - programs that are designed to solve specific problems. And of course, they are all created with code.

Computer and Video Games

Chances are that you've played a computer or video game before. Code is the single most important piece of any computer or video game ever made. In this book, you'll learn how to make a bunch of incredible games of your own that you can play with your family and friends.

More about code

Again, code is just step-by-step instructions that humans write to teach computers how to make things like animations, apps, and games. But you may be wondering...

What does code look like?

Code is written in special languages called **programming languages**. Programming languages are like any other language (i.e. English or Spanish). But instead of using spoken and written words to communicate *ideas* with *people*, programming languages are used to communicated *coded instructions* to *computers*.

Programming languages look like a combination of regular words, special symbols, and simple math.

```
if myHealth <= 0 or monsterHealth <= 0:
    print "GAME OVER"
    break
else:
    monsterMove = random.randint(1,2)
```

There are lots and lots of programming languages out there. For example, JavaScript is used to make websites. Python is often used to create software for robots. And C++ is often used to write instructions for electrical applicances.

Once you've learned how to code in one programming language, it becomes a LOT easier to learn in others!

Where is code written?

Code is written inside of applications called **code editors**. The code editor takes our instructions and translates it into a series of electrical signals that the computer can understand. Finally, the computer takes our translated instructions and does the amazing things we wanted it to do for us in the first place.

if this happens:
    then, do this action
else:
    do this other action

What is Scratch?

Code is written in special languages called programming languages. We also know that we write code inside of special apps called code editors.

This is where Scratch 3 comes in!

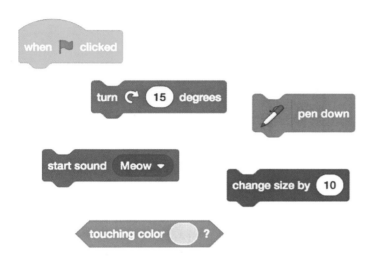

Scratch 3 is both a **programming language** AND a **code editor**. The Scratch language is made of special blocks that each represent one command that we can use in our list of step-by-step instructions. We connect these blocks together like toy bricks.

Different blocks let us do different things. For instance, there are blocks that control motion; blocks that control sound; and blocks that control the appearance of stuff that we see on screen. By using a combination of these code blocks, we can create truly incredible projects!

Is Scratch "real" coding?

Some people think that Scratch isn't "real" coding because it uses blocks instead of typed instructions. But these people are misinformed! Coding in Scratch is just as real as coding in Python. It requires all of the same skills, too: logic, organization, and attention to detail.

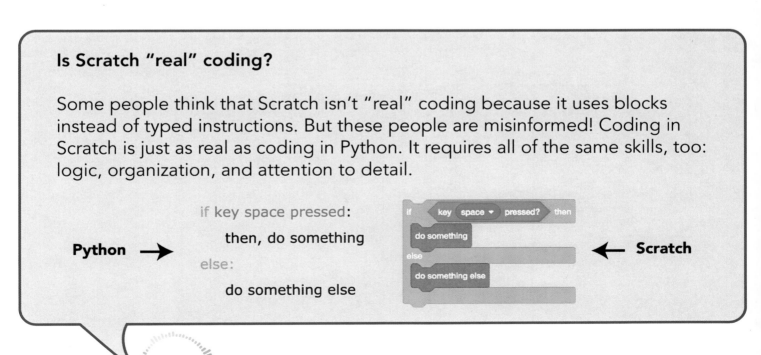

Scratch, the Code Editor

Scratch is also a code editor - a place to write and edit code. The layout takes a little bit of getting used to, but once you know your way around, you'll learn to love how easy and colorful it is to code in Scratch.

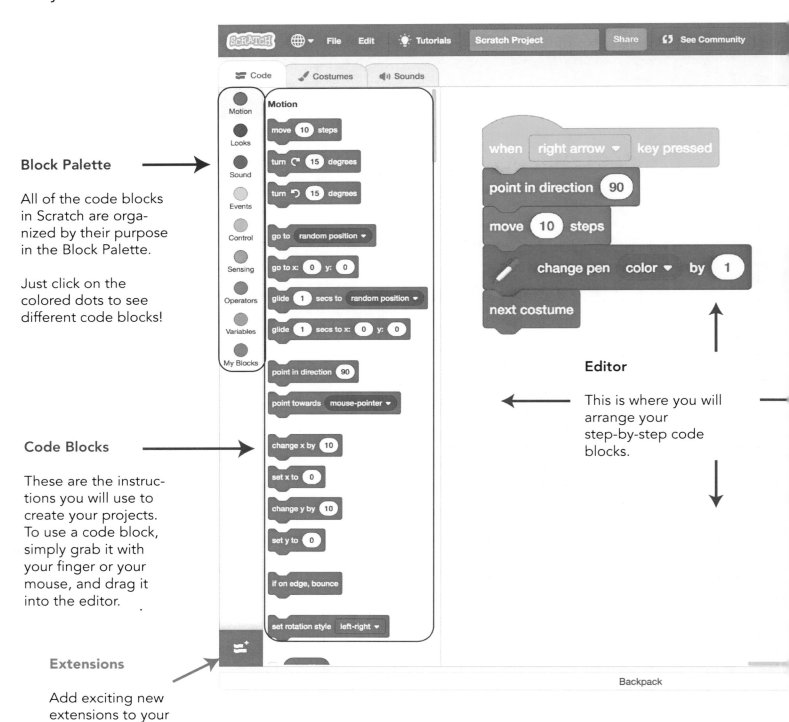

Block Palette

All of the code blocks in Scratch are organized by their purpose in the Block Palette.

Just click on the colored dots to see different code blocks!

Code Blocks

These are the instructions you will use to create your projects. To use a code block, simply grab it with your finger or your mouse, and drag it into the editor.

Extensions

Add exciting new extensions to your code. We'll cover these soon!

Editor

This is where you will arrange your step-by-step code blocks.

User Profile

In just a few pages, you'll create your own Scratch account. This dropdown will let you access your user page.

Change View

Make the stage full screen when you are ready to show off your project.

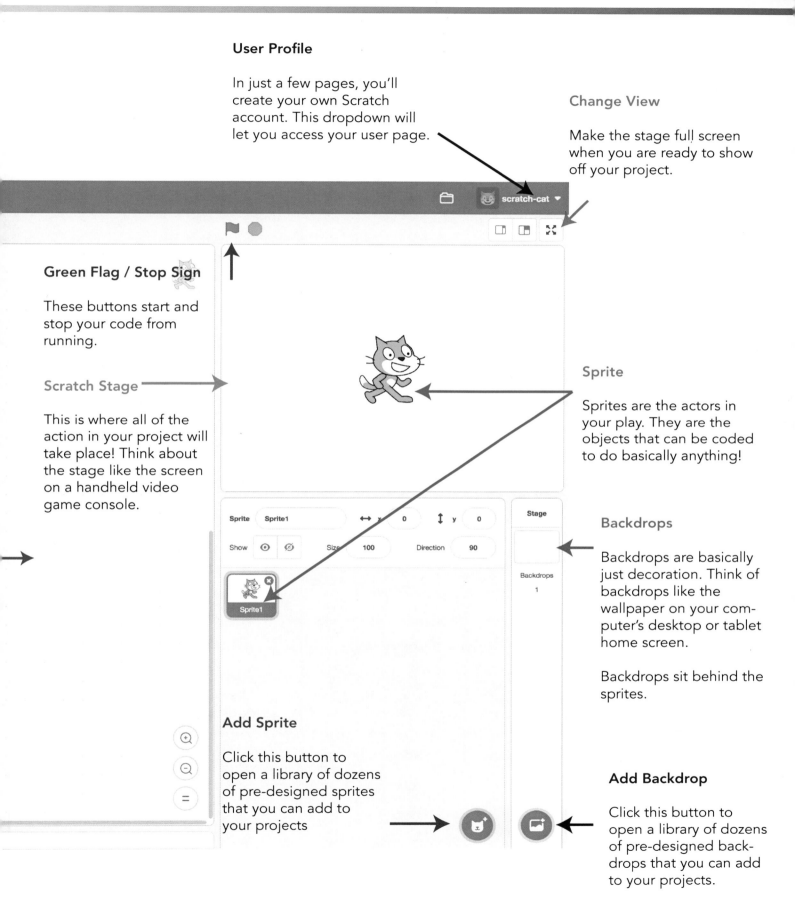

Green Flag / Stop Sign

These buttons start and stop your code from running.

Scratch Stage

This is where all of the action in your project will take place! Think about the stage like the screen on a handheld video game console.

Sprite

Sprites are the actors in your play. They are the objects that can be coded to do basically anything!

Backdrops

Backdrops are basically just decoration. Think of backdrops like the wallpaper on your computer's desktop or tablet home screen.

Backdrops sit behind the sprites.

Add Sprite

Click this button to open a library of dozens of pre-designed sprites that you can add to your projects

Add Backdrop

Click this button to open a library of dozens of pre-designed backdrops that you can add to your projects.

Scratch, the Community

Now we know that Scratch is not just a programming language made up of code blocks, but also a code editor where we can create our own projects.

But did you know that Scratch is also a worldwide community of millions of people and kids like you?

This is one of the most amazing things about Scratch. You can share, collaborate, and connect with kids all over world!

Featured Projects

Scratch allows you to share your projects with the world. And every day, the Scratch team features dozens of projects that they think are interesting from kids just like you.

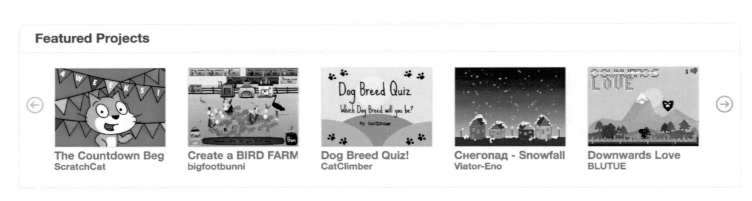

Featured Projects				
The Countdown Beg ScratchCat	Create a BIRD FARM bigfootbunni	Dog Breed Quiz! CatClimber	Снегопад - Snowfall Viator-Eno	Downwards Love BLUTUE

To remix a project, first click "See Inside" on a project you like. That will take you to the project's code editor. Next, in the top right corner, click "Remix"!

Remix Everything!

Scratch also allows you to see projects that other people have shared. Not only can you play with the games and animations they created, you can also see the code they used to make them!

Best of all, you can "remix" almost any project on Scratch. When you remix a project, you create an identical copy of that project and all of its code, allowing you to change or add any code that you like.

Create a Scratch Account, Part I

Grab a computer or tablet - it's time to get started with Scratch!

Follow the steps below to access Scratch. **You will need an adult's help to complete this part**, so ask one to come over and help you

1. Open a Web Browser like Google Chrome, FireFox, or Safari.

2. In the URL bar, type in "scratch.mit.edu"

3. In the top right corner of the Scratch homepage, click "Join Scratch"

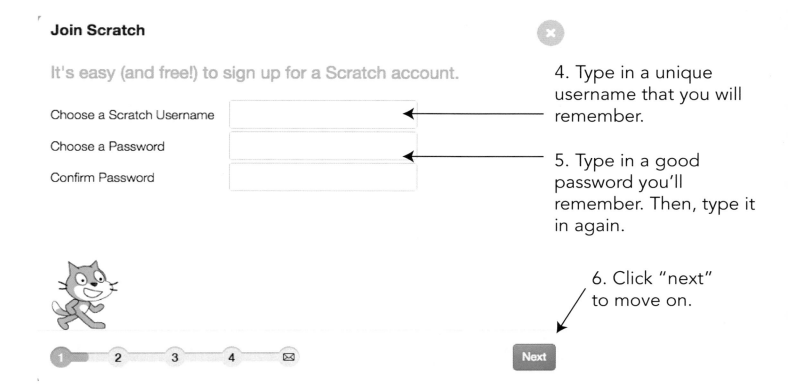

4. Type in a unique username that you will remember.

5. Type in a good password you'll remember. Then, type it in again.

6. Click "next" to move on.

Create a Scratch Account, Part II

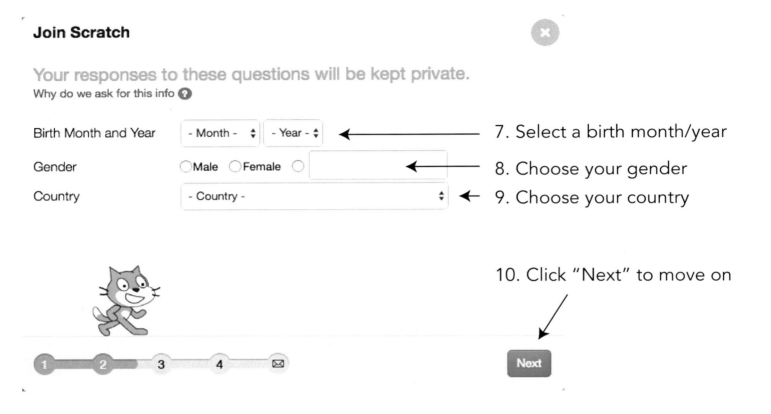

Join Scratch

Your responses to these questions will be kept private.
Why do we ask for this info

Birth Month and Year	- Month - ⬍ - Year - ⬍	←	7. Select a birth month/year
Gender	○Male ○Female ○	←	8. Choose your gender
Country	- Country - ⬍	←	9. Choose your country

10. Click "Next" to move on

Next

Keep your information safe!

Scratch is a very secure and very trustworthy website. However, you should ALWAYS think twice when you are asked to give away information that identifies you (like your name, address, or where you go to school) online.

Remember: your information is valuable. Don't just give it away to any site!

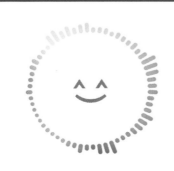

Create a Scratch Account, Part III

Join Scratch   ⊗

Enter your parent's or guardian's email address and we will send
them an email to confirm this account.

Parent's or guardian's email
address

Confirm email address

☐ Receive updates from the
    Scratch Team

11. PARENTS: enter your email
address.

12. Click "Next" to move on.

1 ── 2 ── 3 ── 4 ── ✉   Next

Please confirm this email address by c

Confirm my email address

13. Scratch will have sent you an email to
confirm your/your child's new account. Log
into your email account, find the
confirmation email from Scratch, and click
"Confirm my email address".

Woohoo! You've created your very own Scratch account.

You can now create, save, and share coding projects with the world.

Project #1: Canvas Doggo

Our first Scratch project will also be our silliest. In this application, we'll control Dot the dog using our keyboard arrow keys. As Dot walks up, down, left and right across the stage, he'll leave a trail of rainbow-colored paint everywhere he goes. That lil scamp forgot to clean his paws again!

We'll use our very first code blocks, and learn about the importance of **sequence** - the step-by-step order of our code!

Part 1: Set up the project

1.) Create a new project in Scratch by clicking on the "Create" button in the menu at the top of Scratch.

2.) Click on the 'X' on the Cat Sprite thumbnail to delete it

3.) Click on the "Choose a Sprite" button in the lower right-hand corner

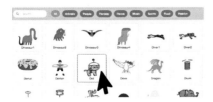

4.) Scroll down until you find the "Dot" dog sprite. Double-click to load it as a Sprite.

Part 1: Set up the project (continued)

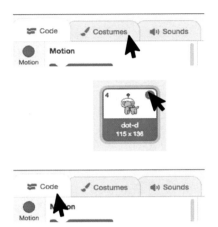

6.) Click on the Costumes tab in the upper left-hand corner

7.) Look on the right side of the screen, and find the 4th costume. Delete this costume by clicking the 'X' in the corner.

8.) Click on the Code tab again.

This project will use blocks that allow us to draw on the Scratch stage. To access those blocks, we have to add the Pen Tool extension.

1.) Click on the "Add Extension" button in the bottom left corner.

2.) Click on the "Pen" box. A Pen tab 🖊 with new pen code blocks will be added to your Block Palette!

Part 2: Code the project

Time to get started! Find the following code blocks from the block palette list, and add them to Dot's code editor in the exact order you see below.

1. Set the starting conditions

This code will put Dot back in the center of the stage, and will also clear away any pen marks that are on the stage.

Click on the tabs in the block palette on the left side of the editor to find these code blocks:

Here's what these blocks do:

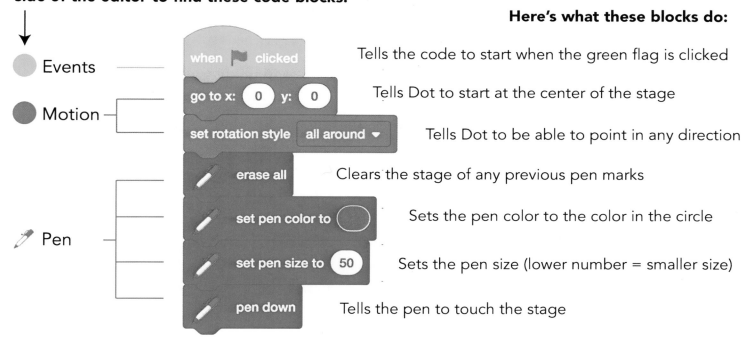

Events

Motion

Pen

when ⚑ clicked — Tells the code to start when the green flag is clicked

go to x: 0 y: 0 — Tells Dot to start at the center of the stage

set rotation style all around ▾ — Tells Dot to be able to point in any direction

erase all — Clears the stage of any previous pen marks

set pen color to ◯ — Sets the pen color to the color in the circle

set pen size to 50 — Sets the pen size (lower number = smaller size)

pen down — Tells the pen to touch the stage

2. Teach Dot to move right and draw

Now it's time to teach Dot how to move around using our arrow keys. First, we'll teach Dot how to move right.

Add the following code next to the code you wrote above in Dot's code editor!

1. Bring out a "When space key pressed" block. Then, use the drowpdown to select "right arrow".

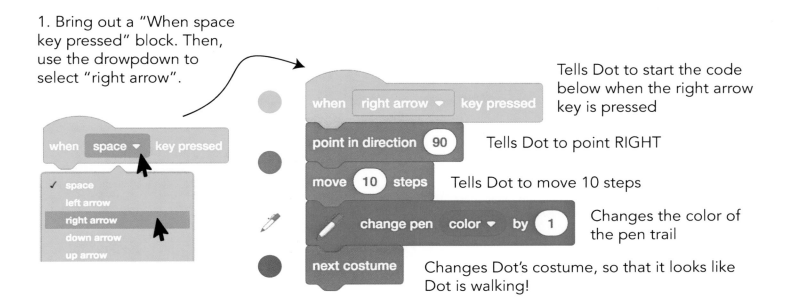

when space ▾ key pressed
✓ space
left arrow
right arrow
down arrow
up arrow

when right arrow ▾ key pressed — Tells Dot to start the code below when the right arrow key is pressed

point in direction 90 — Tells Dot to point RIGHT

move 10 steps — Tells Dot to move 10 steps

change pen color ▾ by 1 — Changes the color of the pen trail

next costume — Changes Dot's costume, so that it looks like Dot is walking!

23

3. Code the instructions to move left, up, and down

Now that Dot knows how to move right, it's easy to teach it to move up, down, and left.

Repeat Step 2 from page 22 to create the following code blocks. Pay close attention to all of the numbers and words with ★ next to them and make sure you change your code blocks to match!

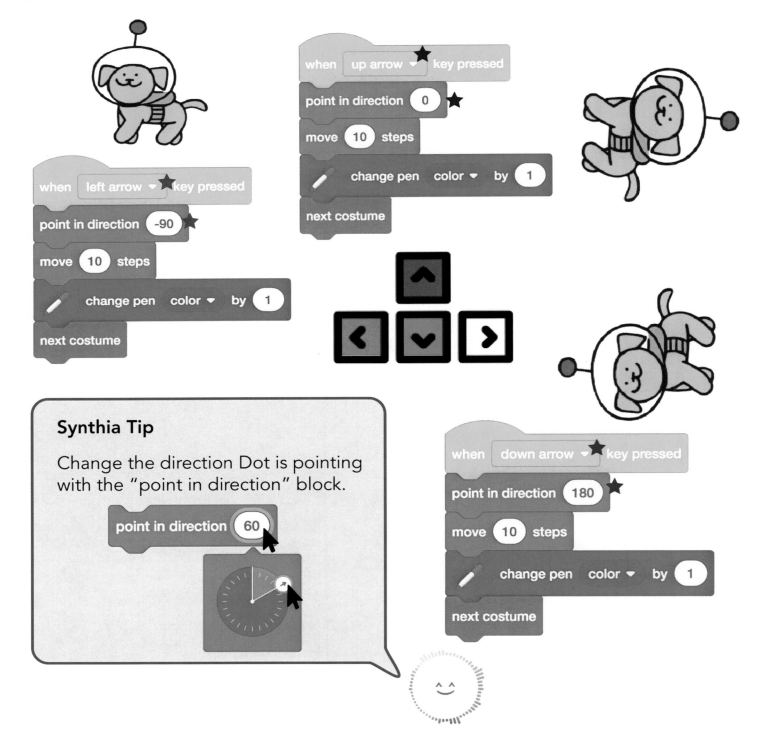

Synthia Tip

Change the direction Dot is pointing with the "point in direction" block.

Part 3: Test your work

Go ahead and click the green flag above the Stage. Can you move Dot around using the arrow keys? Does Dot draw a multicolored line behind itself? When you click the green flag again, do all of the pen marks disappear, and does Dot return to the center of the stage?

If something doesn't seem to be working correctly, study the code from the last few pages very carefully and compare it block by block to your own code. You might find a small error somewhere!

Part 4: Mod your work!

Woohoo! You've built your very first project in Scratch 3. Good job! I'm super duper proudy-pooper of you. Now, it's time to mod your project. "Mod" is just short for "modify". It means to improve the project you just built with your own ideas! Try to accomplish one or more of the following modding challenges:

Challenge 1: Make the pen size thicker.

Challenge 2: Make Dot move faster (hint: change the number in the "move" blocks)

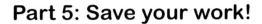

Part 5: Save your work!

Now that you're done with your project, make sure you save a copy of it to your Scratch account.

First, make sure that you're signed in. Use the username and password that you created on page 16 to log in.

Then, at the very top of the code editor, title your project "Canvas Doggo".

Finally, click "File", and then click "Save Now"!

Creates a copy of an already-saved project

Takes you to the folder where all of your saved projects can be found

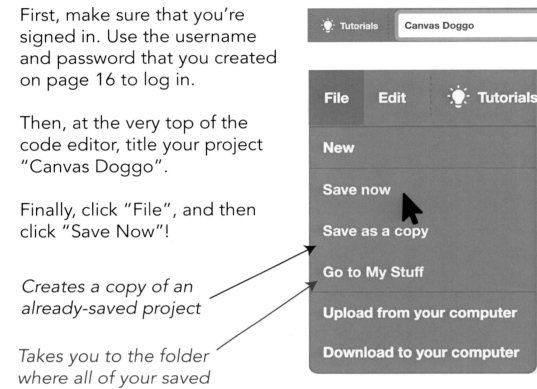

Part 6: Share your work!

By default, your project is totally private - only you can see it and work on its' code.

However, if you would like to show off your work with the world, you'll need to **share** your project. Sharing your project means that anyone on Scratch can see your project, and the Scratch team can showcase it on their homepage.

Additionally, it means that ANYONE can remix your project, allowing them to access the code you wrote for this project.

Chapter 2

Loops

Loops!

We've learned that sequence is the order that code is written. Now, it's time to learn about another important coding concept called Loops.

Loops are often used to create animations. An animation - like the ones you see in movies and on TV - are made by showing a bunch of still images one after the other. When this is done really fast, then it looks like the characters are really moving!

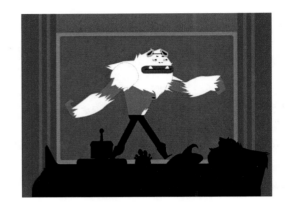

When we create animations, we will have to repeat the same instructions - like showing our sprite's next costume - over and over and over again. For example, a 30-second animation is made up of 1,800 still images. Put another way, that's 1,800 "next costume" code blocks!

That's the problem: dragging out the same code block 1,800 times would be way. Too. Much. WORK!

Luckily, we can use special code blocks called **Loops** to make this go a lot faster. **A loop is a type of code block that allows us to repeat the same command as many times as we want.**

There are two very common types of loops that we'll use in most of our coding projects: **repeat loops**, and **forever loops**.

Repeat Loops allow us to tell the computer exactly how many times we want to repeat the code blocks inside of the loop. For example, we might want the following code blocks to repeat 10 times.

By the end of it, the sprite that this repeat loop was written on will have:

- moved 100 steps
- turned 150 degrees
- increased in size by 50

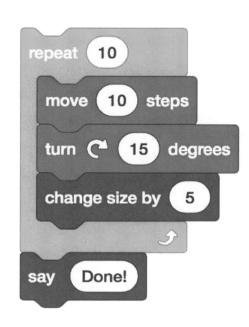

Finally, the "Say (Done!)" block attached to the bottom of the repeat loop will not run until the loop has completed all 10 repetitions.

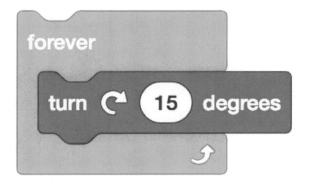

On the other hand, **Forever Loops** have no limit on how many times they will repeat the instructions inside of them. Once our computer reaches a forever block, it will repeat the instructions inside of them forever - or, at least until the program is stopped.

So, the code to the left will make the sprite spin around in a circle forever.

Nothing can be attached under a forever loop, because the program will never be able to complete an infinity of repetitions!

Project #2: Dino Dance Battle

The age of the dinosaurs was a terrifying one indeed, with fierce, gargantuan lizards that hunted one another and fought for domination of their jurassic lands. But we bet you didn't know that they also loved to dance together to the tune of sick beats (**paleontologist's note:** *they did **not** do this to our scientific knowledge*)!

In this fun animation, you'll code up a scene of a couple of dancing dinos. You'll learn how to add sound and songs into Scratch, also how to use loops to animate your sprites. Let's get dancin'!

Backdrop: Jurassic

Sprite: Dinosaur2

Sprite: Dinosaur4

Part 1: Set up the project

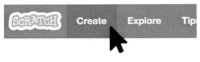

1.) Create a new project in Scratch

2.) Delete the Cat sprite

3.) Click on the "Choose a Sprite" button

4.) Scroll down until you find the "Dinosaur2" sprite. Click on it to add it as a new sprite.

5.) Click on the "Choose a Sprite" button again

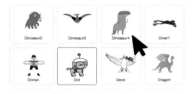

6.) Scroll down until you find the "Dinosaur4" sprite. Click on it to add it as a new sprite.

7.) Click on the "Choose a Backdrop" button

8.) Scroll down until you find "Jurassic". Click on it to load it as a new backdrop.

9.) You will be taken to the backdrop editor screen. To go to Dinosaur4's code editor again, click on its sprite thumbnail

10.) Click on the Code tab

Part 2: Code the project

Time to get started! Find the following code blocks, then add them to Dinosaur4's code editor in the exact order you see below.

1. Arrange the dinosaurs on the stage

First, arrange your sprites so that Dinosaur4 is on the left, and Dinosaur2 is on the right. Do this by clicking on each sprite and dragging it into the correct position.

You will notice that Dinosaur2 is pointing the wrong way, but don't worry - we'll fix that in a bit.

2. Set the starting conditions for Dinosaur4

Make sure you have Dinosaur4 selected. In this animation, both dinosaurs will change position, constumes, and also change color. So, whenever this animation restarts, we want to make sure the dinosaurs start in the correct position, with their 1st costume, and with their normal coloring.

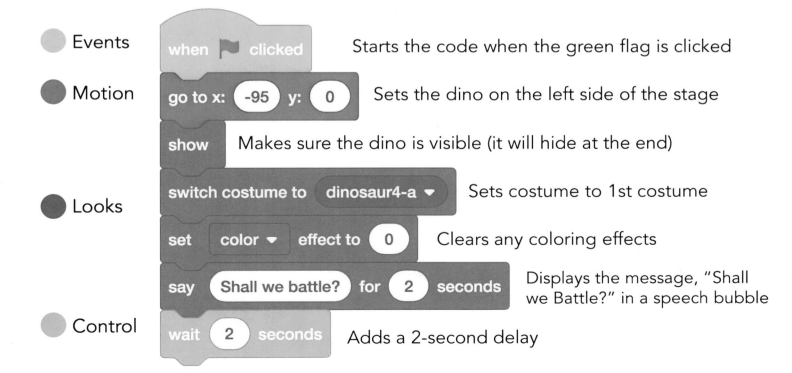

- **Events** — when 🏳 clicked — Starts the code when the green flag is clicked
- **Motion** — go to x: -95 y: 0 — Sets the dino on the left side of the stage
- show — Makes sure the dino is visible (it will hide at the end)
- **Looks** — switch costume to dinosaur4-a ▾ — Sets costume to 1st costume
- set color ▾ effect to 0 — Clears any coloring effects
- say Shall we battle? for 2 seconds — Displays the message, "Shall we Battle?" in a speech bubble
- **Control** — wait 2 seconds — Adds a 2-second delay

3. Keep coding Dinosaur 4

Now that Dinosaur4 knows what to do at the start of the project, let's teach it how to dance! To dance, each dino will first change to its next costume, then change color, then freeze for .25 seconds. It will **repeat** those 3 steps 60 times.

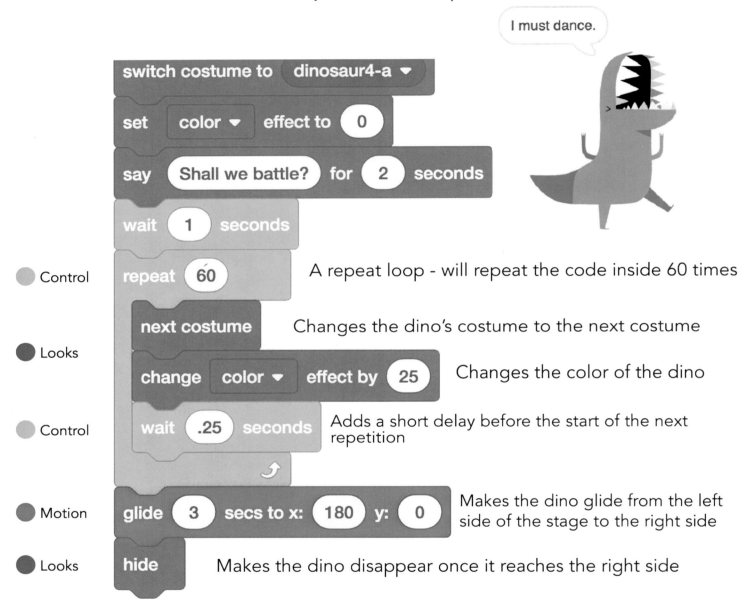

I must dance.

Control — A repeat loop - will repeat the code inside 60 times

Looks — Changes the dino's costume to the next costume

Changes the color of the dino

Control — Adds a short delay before the start of the next repetition

Motion — Makes the dino glide from the left side of the stage to the right side

Looks — Makes the dino disappear once it reaches the right side

4. Test your work

Click the green flag to test your work. Does the dinosaur start on the left side of the stage? Does it say "Let's Battle."? Does it repeat its dance steps 60 times? Does it glide to the right side of the stage, then disappear?

5. Code Dinosaur2

Dinosaur2's code will be very similar to Dinosaur4's. Click on Dinosaur2 to get started. Then, bring out the following code.

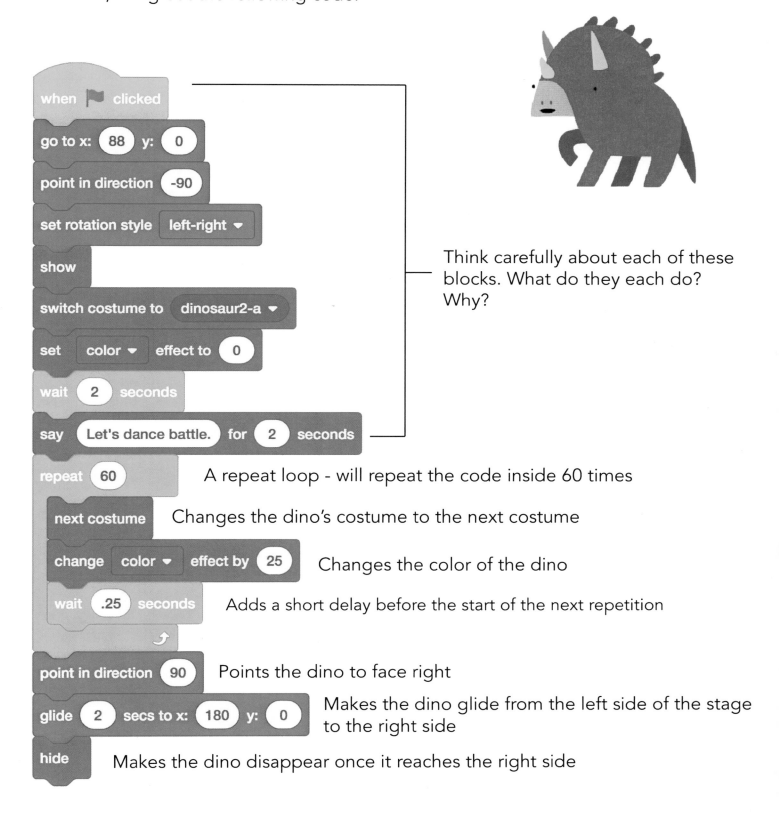

Think carefully about each of these blocks. What do they each do? Why?

A repeat loop - will repeat the code inside 60 times

Changes the dino's costume to the next costume

Changes the color of the dino

Adds a short delay before the start of the next repetition

Points the dino to face right

Makes the dino glide from the left side of the stage to the right side

Makes the dino disappear once it reaches the right side

6. Add sound to your project

What's a dance battle without music? An awkward dance battle, that's what! So let's get these dinos grooving to a fun tune.

To use sounds in Scratch, you first need to load them into your project.

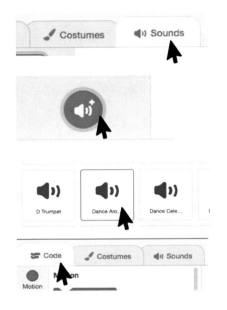

1.) Click on the Sounds tab in the upper left-hand corner

2.) Click the "Choose a Sound" button in the bottom left.

3.) Scroll down until you find the sound file labeled "Dance Around". Then click to load it into your project.

4.) Click on the Code tab again to return to the code editor.

7. Cue the music

Now that we've added the sound file to the project, it's time to code the instructions for when it should start playing. We want it to start playing immediately after the dinosaurs are done talking.

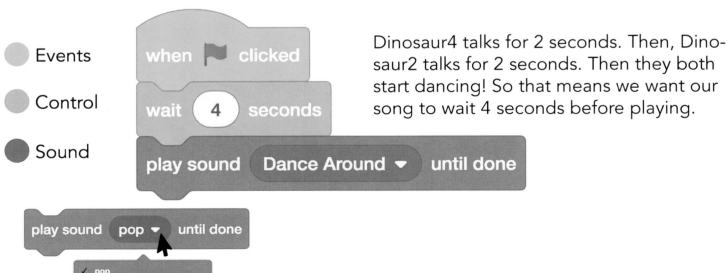

Dinosaur4 talks for 2 seconds. Then, Dinosaur2 talks for 2 seconds. Then they both start dancing! So that means we want our song to wait 4 seconds before playing.

Part 3: Test your work

Click the green flag to test your work.

- Are the dinos in their proper positions?
- Do both dinos talk, one after the other?
- Do they both dance for the same amount of time?
- Is your music track working?
- Do the dinos chase each other across the stage, then disappear?

Part 4: Mod your work!

Hey, that was fun! You learned how to use loops, sound files, and visual effects to create a fun animation. Now, it's time to mod your project!

Challenge 1: Make the dinos dance twice as long (hint: look at the number of repeats)

Challenge 2: Make the music file play twice as long

Challenge 3: Put forever loops around each dino's repeat loops to see what happens

Project #3: Google Translate

One of Google's earlier and most exciting applications was Google Translate. With Google Translate, you could translate any word or phrase into basically any other language spoken on Earth. Meaning that if you wanted to see what "Where are my pants?!" looks like in German, you now could (*Wo sind meine Hosen?!*)! With Scratch 3, we now have access to a fully functional translator, so now we can build our very own version of Google Translate. Amazing!

The Google sprite asks the user to enter any phrase or word...

The user types the phrase into a special box that accepts user input

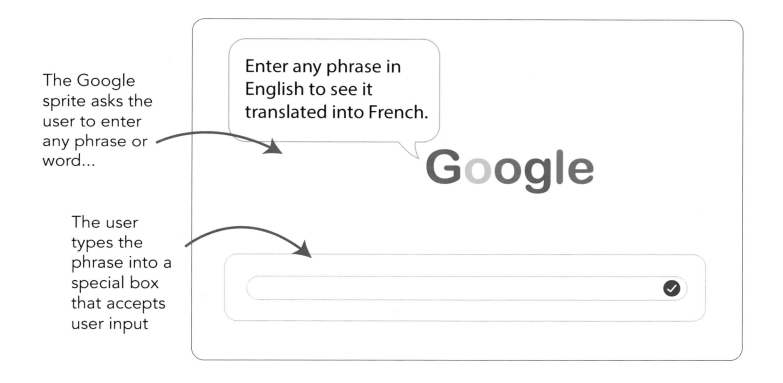

Enter any phrase in English to see it translated into French.

We don't need any sprites or backdrops from Scratch's library for this project. Instead, we'll draw our own "Google" sprite. Flip the page to learn how!

Part 1: Set up the project

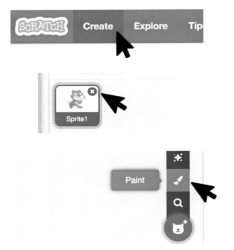

1.) Create a new project in Scratch

2.) Delete the Cat Sprite

3.) In this project, we'll be drawing our own sprite instead of using one from the library. So, hover your mouse over the "Choose a Sprite" button, and then click "Paint".

Part 2: Explore the Costume Editor

Let's explore the basics of Scratch 3's costume editor. This window has every tool we need to draw our very own sprites.

The **Pointer Tool** allows you to grab and move drawn objects around the window.

The **Line, Circle, and Rectangle** tools allow you to draw those shapes.

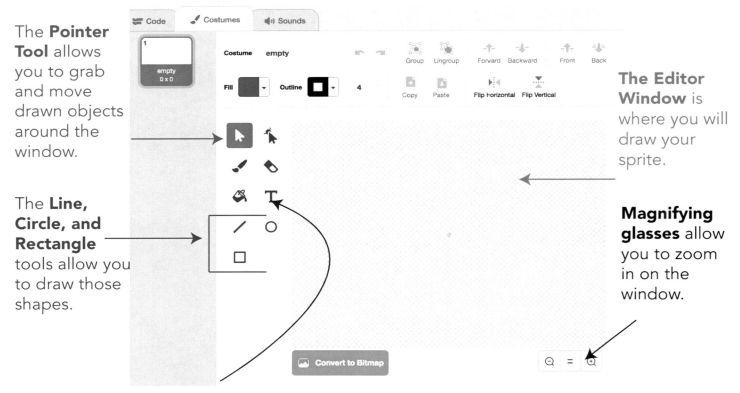

The Editor Window is where you will draw your sprite.

Magnifying glasses allow you to zoom in on the window.

The **Text Tool** allows you to add words to your sprite drawings.

Google

1. Draw a Google logo sprite

Our sprite will be the Google logo. We could always find an image of the Google logo online, but sometimes it's better to draw your own in Scratch so that you can do fun effects to it later.

1. Click on the Type Tool on the left side of the costume editor.

2. Click anywhere in the Editor window to create a text box. A text box is just a box that will hold the words or letters we type.

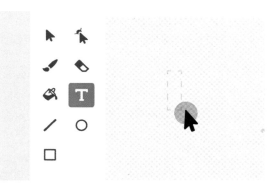

3. Now, with your keyboard, type a capital letter G inside of your new text box.

4. Now, create another text box next to the first one. We need to make one text box for each letter in 'Google' so that we can make each letter a different color.

Type the letter 'o' into this new text box.

5. Repeat Steps 2-4 to add the rest of the letters in the word 'Google'

6. Now, it's time to color in our logo. Make sure that the first letter 'G' is selected. Then, look above the Editor window to see the color box with the word 'Fill' next to it.

This tool allows us to change the color of a shape our of our letters.

7. A menu will appear with a few sliders on it that let us get exactly the color we want.

Play around with the sliders until you get a color of blue that you like for the 'G'!

8. Repeat Step 7 for each letter in the logo. Use the color selector to color in each letter like you see to the left.

9. Woohoo! We're done creating our Google logo. It's a little small right now - we should make it bigger before we start on our code.

First, click on the Pointer tool.

10. Now, use your mouse to draw a box around ALL of the letters. Do this by clicking in the Editor window, then holding down the mouse key and drawing a box.

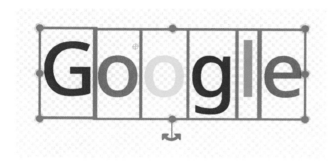

You should now see each letter with a solid blue line around it.

You'll also see a bunch of circles around the outlines of the letters. These are called **anchor points**. They let us stretch our sprite in any direction.

With your mouse, click on the bottom right anchor point. Keep your mouse clicked down, then pull it diagonally down.

This will make ALL of the letters get evenly bigger.

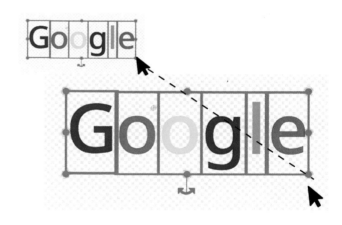

Good job! You just made your first custom sprite! It can now be coded just like any sprite from the Scratch library.

To finish up, click on the Code tab to go to the sprite code editor.

Part 3: Code the project

Time to get started! Find the following code blocks from the block palette list, and add them to your Google logo sprite's code editor.

1. Ask the user to enter a phrase

In this project, the user - the person using the app you are making - can enter any phrase in English and see it translated into French. That means that we need a way for the user to type in a phrase and send it to our app. Luckily, the is `ask What's your name? and wait` a very handy block we can use to get input from our users.

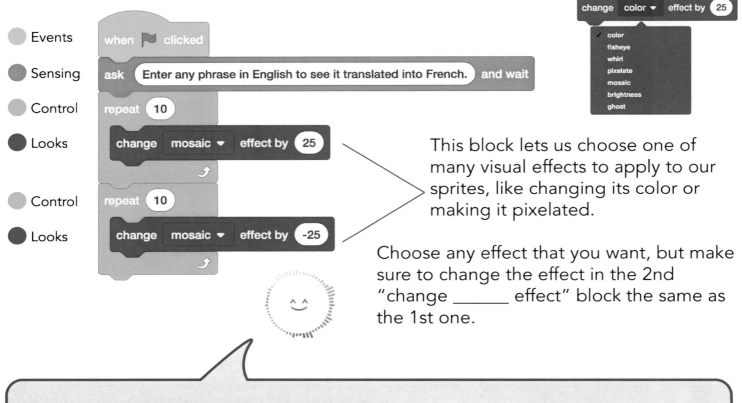

This block lets us choose one of many visual effects to apply to our sprites, like changing its color or making it pixelated.

Choose any effect that you want, but make sure to change the effect in the 2nd "change _____ effect" block the same as the 1st one.

Synthia Tip: The Ask and Answer blocks

The "ask" block can be found in the Sensing tab. This is a very special block that allows the person using your app to send text to your app. The text that the user sends is held inside of the "answer" block, which is also found in the Sensing tab.

2. Repeat the repeats

Let's make the visual effect that we programmed in the last step repeat itself 5 times. To do that, we can put the repeat loops we just created *inside of another repeat loop*!

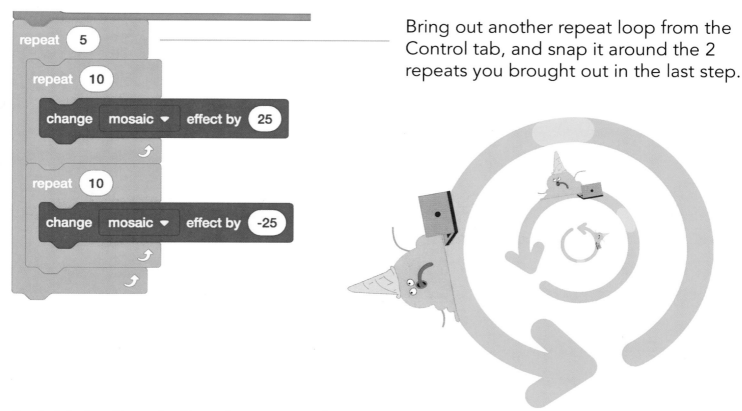

Bring out another repeat loop from the Control tab, and snap it around the 2 repeats you brought out in the last step.

3. Add the Google Translate extension

Scratch 3 has some pretty cool extensions. You've already used the Pen Extension in the Canvas Doggo project. Now you're going to use the Google Translate Extension!

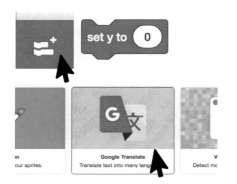

1.) Click on the "Add Extension" button in the bottom left corner

2.) Select "Google Translate". This will add a new tab to our Block Palette with new code blocks.

4. Translate the user's text

Now it's time to translate the text that the user entered at the beginning of the project. To do so, we need to **combine** 3 blocks into 1 block.

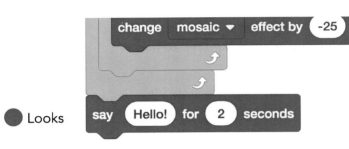

1. Attach this block *underneath* all of your repeat blocks. We will use this block to show a message to the user.

2. Bring out this block from the new Translate tab. This block will change some text from English into almost any other language!

translate hello to Malayalam ▼

3. Next, take the translate block you just brought out and snap it inside of the "Say Hello!" block.

To do that, just hold the block over where it says "Hello" in the purple block. You should see the purple block stretch to fit the new green block.

4. Bring out an "answer" block from the ● Sensing tab. Remember that the "answer" block is holding onto the text that the user entered from the "ask" block that we added in the first step.

answer

5. Finally, snap the "answer" block into the "translate" block where it says "hello".

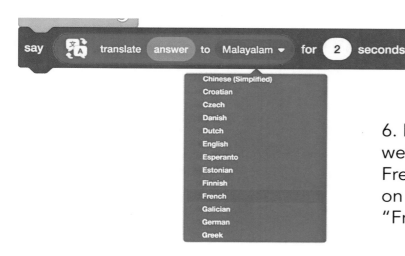

6. Next, we need to change the language we're translating the user's answer into to French. To do so, click on the white arrow on the "translate" block, and find "French" from the menu that appears.

7. Finally, let's display the translation to the user for 5 seconds instead of 2 seconds.

5. Test your work

Click the green flag to test your work.

- Does your Google logo ask you to enter a phrase in English?
- Does your logo animate the way you wanted it to?
- Does the phrase you entered get translated into French?
- Is it shown for 5 seconds?

If your project is working perfectly so far, good job! Otherwise, go back and make sure you didn't miss any steps.

Good job! Your project is working perfectly. But isn't it kind of annoying how you have to keep pressing the green flag to start the program over and translate another phrase?

Wouldn't it be better if the app translated one phrase, then automatically asked us if we wanted to translate another phrase?

Remember the Forever Loop? This block is similar to the Repeat Loop, but instead of looping a certain number of times (like 5, 10, or 1498), the Forever Loop repeats the instructions inside of it forever - or at least as long as our user is using our app!

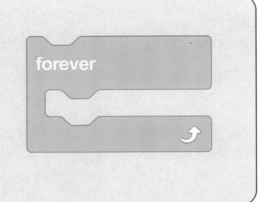

1. To make our app automatically ask us if we want to translate another phrase after it translates the last phrase we entered, bring out a "Forever" loop from the ● Control tab.

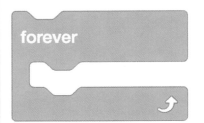

2. Next, wrap it around ALL of the code underneath the "When green flag clicked" block.

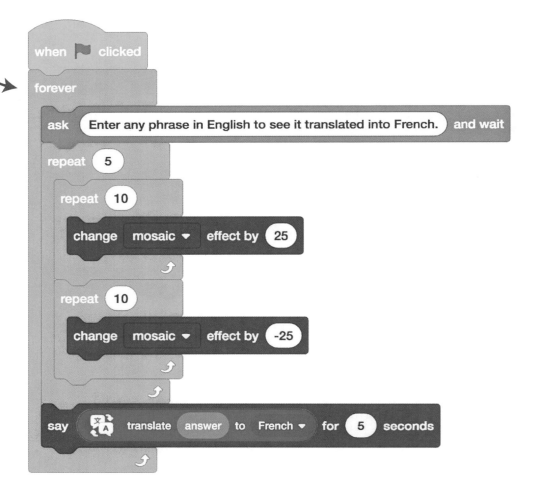

Part 4: Test your work

Click the green flag to test your work.

- Does your app now automatically ask you for another phrase to translate after the first one?

Part 5: Mod your work

Amazing job, coder! You learned how to draw your own sprites, use the Google Translate extension, and use a Forever Loop to make your app repeat its instructions for as long as someone is using it. Now, it's time to mod your project!

First, SAVE your work. Then, create a COPY of your project so that you always have a clean, unmodified backup to go back to.

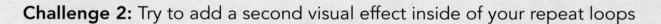

Challenge 1: Try to make the logo move slowly around the stage

Challenge 2: Try to add a second visual effect inside of your repeat loops

Challenge 3: Make it so that the user's phrase is translated into more than one language!

Chapter 3

If-Then Statements

IF I'm hungry...

grumble   grumble

Presto
Pasto!

THEN eat a taco!

If-Then Statements

Listen up, coders! You're about to learn how to teach your programs to make simple decisions using **If-Then Statements**.

An If-Then Statement is a way for us to decide if we need to do something or not.

You know how to make tons of simple decisions using If-Then Statements already. Like, "**IF something is hot, THEN don't touch it.**" Or, "**IF it is raining, THEN bring an umbrella.**"

Let's break down each piece of an if-then statement:

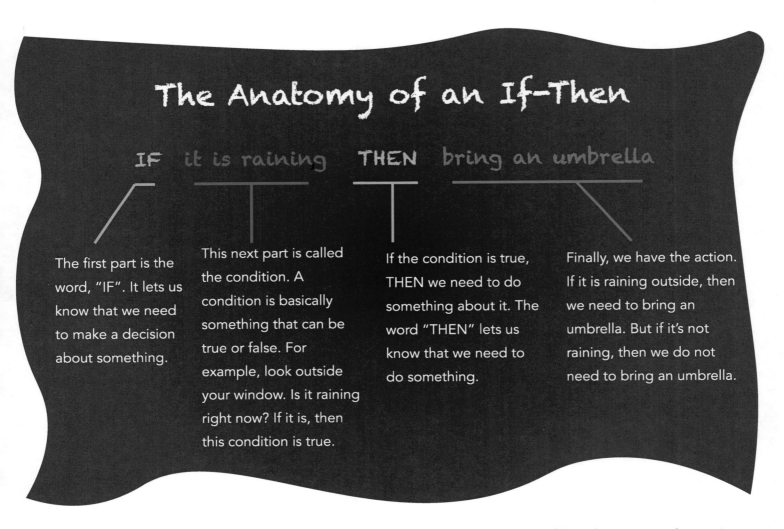

The Anatomy of an If-Then

IF   it is raining   THEN   bring an umbrella

The first part is the word, "IF". It lets us know that we need to make a decision about something.

This next part is called the condition. A condition is basically something that can be true or false. For example, look outside your window. Is it raining right now? If it is, then this condition is true.

If the condition is true, THEN we need to do something about it. The word "THEN" lets us know that we need to do something.

Finally, we have the action. If it is raining outside, then we need to bring an umbrella. But if it's not raining, then we do not need to bring an umbrella.

Can you come up with 5 more examples of If-Then Statements like the ones above?

As we code more advanced computer programs, we will need our programs to make simple decisions by themselves, too! For example, we might want the program to move a sprite to the right **IF** the right arrow key on our keyboards gets pressed. In this case, the computer program has to check if the right arrow key is pressed. **IF** it is, **THEN** it will decide to move our sprite to the right.

Or, we might want the computer program to end the game **IF** our health reaches 0. In this case, the computer program has to check if our health is equal to 0. **IF** it is, **THEN** it will decide to end the game.

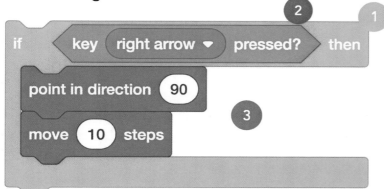

In Scratch, every If-Then statement has the same three pieces:

1. The if-then block

2. A "condition" block (something can be true or false).

3. The action(s) the program should do if the condition is true.

Project #4: Free Kick

The World Cup only comes once every four years. But we bet you can't get enough soccer in your life, so that's why we're going to build ourselves a free kick game! This is going to be a multiplayer game, meaning that two people can play. Player 1 will control the goalie, moving it left-to-right to try and block Player 2 from scoring a goal with the soccer ball! If the ball hits the goalie, then it bounces back towards Player 2. But if it sneaks past the goalie, then it's a GOOOOOALLLL!!!!!!

Player 1 controls the goalie. They Can move goalie side to side using A and D keys on the keyboard.

Player 2 controls the soccer ball. Can move soccer ball left and right using the mouse. Can shoot the soccer ball by clicking with the mouse.

Part 1: Set up the project

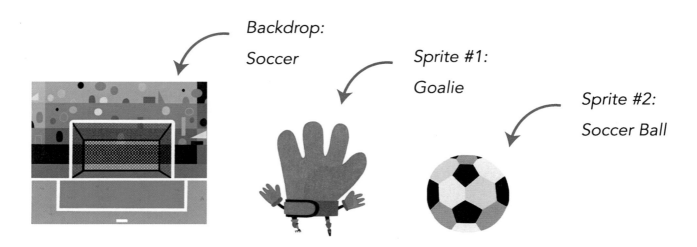

Backdrop:

Soccer

Sprite #1:

Goalie

Sprite #2:

Soccer Ball

Part 2: Code the Goalie

Time to get started! Make sure you have selected your goalie sprite and are working on its code editor. Then, start adding the code below.

1. Initialize the Goalie

Let's start by adding code that will set the Goalie's size, where it starts on the stage, and its rotation style (how it moves left to right).

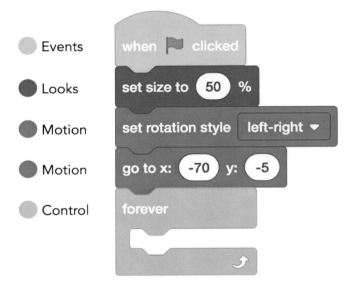

Remember, this block just stops the Goalie from flipping over when it changes direction.

2. Teach the Goalie to move right

Great job! Our next step is to write code that will let someone playing the game move the Goalie right using the 'd' key on the keyboard. To do so, we need our program to first check IF the 'd' key is pressed.

1. Bring out an "if-then" block from the ● Control tab.

2. Then, snap it inside of the "forever" loop.

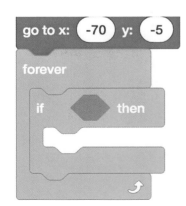

Now that we have an if-then block, we need to add a condition. Remember that the condition can be TRUE or FALSE. If its true, then the program will do the thing we want it to. If it's false, then it won't!

Here, our condition is simply, "Is the 'd' key pressed?"

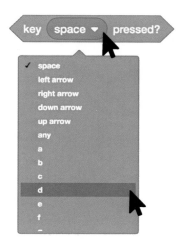

3. Bring out a "key space pressed?" block from the ● Sensing tab. Then, use the dropdown arrow to select 'd'.

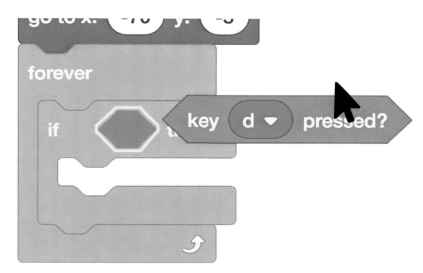

4. Next, drag the "key 'd' pressed?" block into the diamond-shaped cut-out on the "if-then" block.

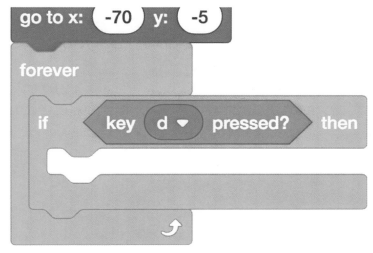

You'll know the block is ready to snap in when the cut-out glows with a white border.

Finally, we need to add the action that the program will take IF the 'd' key is pressed. Remember: we want the Goalie to move right!

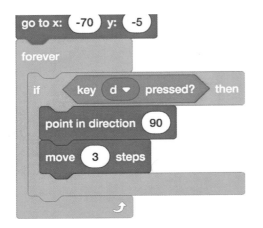

5. From the ● Motion tab, bring out these two blocks. The "point in direction" block will point the Goalie to the right. And the "move 3 steps" block will actually move it in that direction.

3. Teach the Goalie to move left

Nice! Next, it's time to teach the Goalie to move left. Follow the directions from the last few steps to write an if-then block that moves the Goalie left when the 'a' key is pressed.

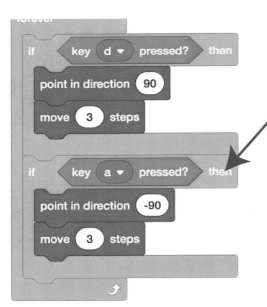

1. Put a new if-then block under the first one
2. Bring out a new condition (key 'a' pressed?) block
3. Snap it inside of the if-then block
4. Add the motion blocks to make the Goalie move left
5. Make sure to change the direction from 90 to -90

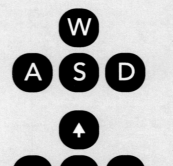

Have you ever noticed how some multiplayer computer games use the W, A, S, and D keys for the second player?

It's because these keys are basically arranged in the same pattern as the up, down, left, and right arrow keys, which the first player is probably using.

4. Test your work

- Does the Goalie start in the bottom left corner of the goal?
- Does it move to the right if you press 'd'?
- Does it move to the left if you press 'a'?
- Does it stay right-side up when you move it left?

Part 3: Code the Ball

Well done, coder! You've successfully used if-then statements to teach your program to make decisions. Now, you will need to use a few more of them to complete the code for the Ball sprite.

1. Make sure you have clicked on your Ball sprite and are coding in its editor.

Then, bring out the code you see to the right to set its starting position and size.

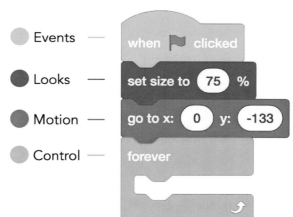

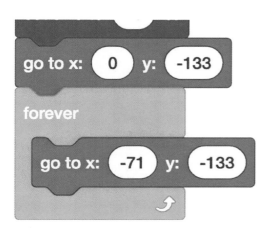

2. Instead of using the keyboard to move the ball left and right, Player 2 will use the mouse. Wherever the player's mouse moves, the Ball should follow it.

From the ● Motion tab, bring out the "go to x: y:" block and put it inside of the forever loop.

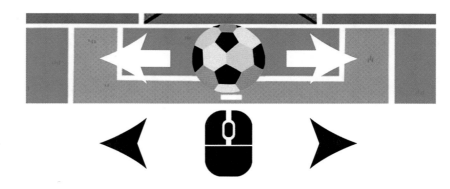

The Ball should only follow your mouse's left and right movement. We don't want it to follow the mouse up and down!

So, from the ⬤ Sensing tab, bring out a "mouse x" block. Then, snap it into the x-position of the "go to" block.

1

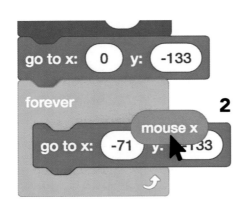

2

3

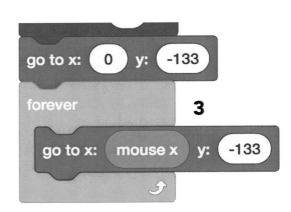

Synthia Tip: X and Y

In all of the projects we've done so far, we've used blocks that use the terms "x" and "y". What do these letters *mean* though?

Simply put, "X" is just another word for left-right movement, or position. "Y" is just another word for up-down movement or position. The bigger the "X" value, the further right it is. And the bigger the "Y" value, the further up it is.

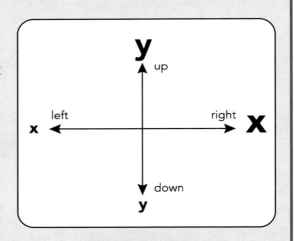

The "mouse x" block that you just used basically tracks the left-right position of your mouse pointer at all times. So, when we dropped it into the "go to x:( ) y:(-133)" block inside of the forever loop, that means the Ball sprite will always follow the left-right position of your mouse.

Now that the Ball follows the mouse, let's teach it to launch towards the goal when the mouse **is clicked.**

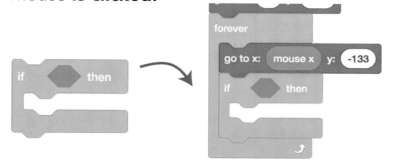

1. Bring out an if-then block from the ⬤ Control tab, and put it inside of the forever loop, underneath the "go to" block.

2. From the ⬤ Sensing tab, bring out a "mouse down?" block. Snap it inside of the if-then block's diamond-shaped condition cut-out.

The "mouse down?" block is used to check whether the mouse is clicked.

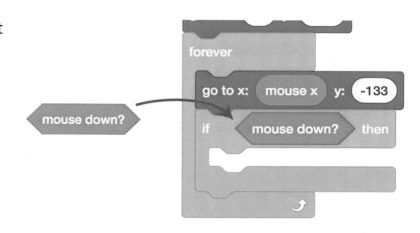

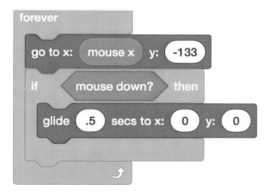

3. Next, from the ⬤ Motion tab, bring out a "glide (1) secs to x:( ) y:( )" block and snap it inside of the if-then block.

Change the number of seconds the glide should last to .5.

Change the "y" value (up-down) to 0.

4. Finally, from the ⬤ Operators tab, bring out the "pick random (1) to (10)" block. Snap this block inside of the "x" field on the "glide" block.

Change the numbers in the "pick random" block to -80 and 80.

This block will now choose a random "x" value (left-right) between -80 and 80 for our soccer ball to glide to.

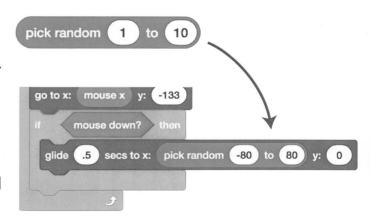

2. Test your work

Click the green flag and test your work:

- Does the Ball follow the left-right movement of your mouse?
- When you click with your mouse, does the Ball shoot towards the goal?
- Does the Ball pick a random spot in the goal to shoot towards?
- Does the Ball return back to its original position after it hits the goal?

3. The Goalie saves!

Now that our Goalie can move and our Ball can be kicked, let's write the code that will make the Ball bounce away IF the Goalie touches it in time.

Make sure that you are still coding on your Ball sprite. Then:

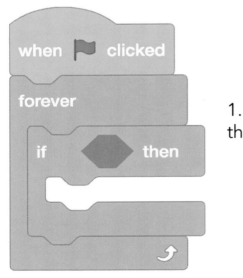

1. Bring out all the blocks you see to the left, and arrange them somewhere below all of the code you wrote in Step 5.

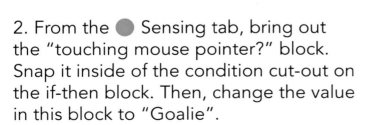

2. From the ● Sensing tab, bring out the "touching mouse pointer?" block. Snap it inside of the condition cut-out on the if-then block. Then, change the value in this block to "Goalie".

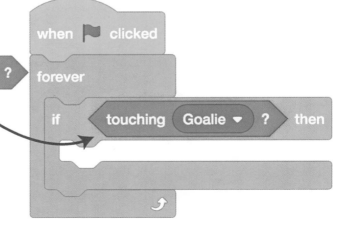

Our new code on the Ball sprite is now checking to see whether the Ball is touching the Goalie. Let's give the Ball an action to do IF that condition is true.

IF the Ball sprite touches the Goalie Sprite, THEN we want the Ball to glide back to a random "x" position, making it seem like the Goalie actually knocked it back to the kicker.

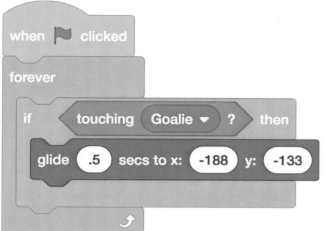

3. From the ● Motion tab, bring out another "glide to x: ( ) y: ( )" block. Attach it inside of the if-then block.

Make sure that the number of seconds that the glide lasts is changed to .5. Also make sure that the "y" value is -133.

4. Next, from the ● Operator tab, bring out another "pick random 1 to 10" block. Snap it inside of the "x" field on the "glide" block. Then, change the numbers in the "pick random" block to (-100) to (100).

Can you guess what this will do?

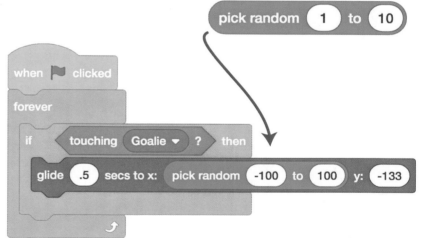

Click the green flag and try kicking the ball a few times. What happens when it hits the Goalie? It should glide back down to the starting position, but in a random left-right place!

DENIED!!!

smack!

4. The Ball scores!!!

Nice! Now that we've finished coding the instructions for what should happen if the Ball touches the Goalie on its way to the goal, let's move on to what should happen if the Goalie *misses* the Ball.

Here's how this will work: IF the Ball touches the Goalie, THEN it will immediately glide back to its starting position. But if it does NOT touch the Goalie, then it should keep traveling up towards the goal.

To decide if the Ball has scored a goal, we want to check if tits "y" position is greater than a certain number.

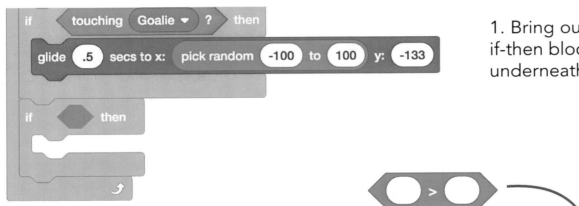

1. Bring out another if-then block, and place it underneath the first one.

2. From the ● Operators tab, bring out a "( ) > ( )" block. Snap it inside of the new if-then block.

This block is a "greater than" block. On each side, there will be a number. The block will check to see if the 1st number is greater than the 2nd number. If it is, then the program will do the action below it.

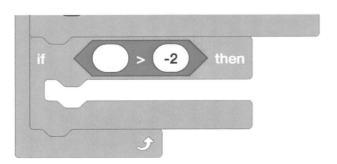

3. Click in the 2nd box in the greater-than block. Then, type in "-2".

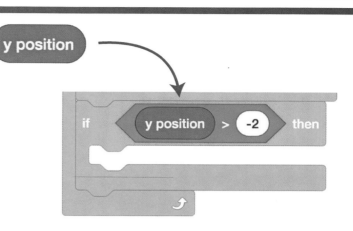

4. Now, from the ● Motion tab, bring out a "y position" block. Snap it into the 1st box in the greater-than block.

The "y position" block tracks the up-down value of the Ball sprite. It will let us check where the Ball is at any given second.

Goooalll!!!

No goal below the yellow line...

When the player clicks the mouse to shoot the Ball to the goal, the Ball sprite is basically just moving UPWARDS on the Scratch stage.

The code that we just did is constantly checking to see IF the Ball sprite's current height is higher than (greater than) a "y" value of -2.

Think of the -2 as an invisible yellow line. If the Ball is anywhere *below* that yellow line, then it *has not* scored. But if it is *above* that line, then it *has* scored!

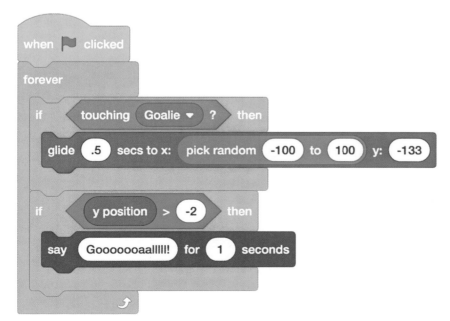

5. Final step! From the ● Looks tab, bring out a "Say 'Hello!' for 2 secs" block and snap it inside of your last if-then block.

Change the text in this "say" block to "Goooooooaaalllll!"

Then, change the number of seconds (secs) this message is displayed for to 1.

Part 4: Test your work

Click the green flag and test your work:

- If the Ball touches the Goalie, is it deflected back?
- If the Goalie misses the Ball, does the Ball say "Gooooallll!"?

Part 5: Mod your work

Congratulations on making your first computer game, coder! Not only did you learn to use if-then statements to help make your program make choices, but you also succeeded in making a multiplayer computer game. Seriously - have you coded before or something?! You're a pro!

Save your work, then make a copy of the Free Kick project so that you can mod one copy without losing your original work.

Challenge 1: Add a cheering sound when the Ball scores

Challenge 2: Create a 1-player version of the game where the Goalie automatically moves from side to side

Project #5: Taco Wiz

Tacos are a delicious, magical food, and nobody knows that better than hungry computer-wizards. In this project, we'll build a game where magical tacos falldown from the sky like tasty rain. Meanwhile, our player will control the wizard sprite with their left and right arrow keys, trying to grab each taco before it hits the ground. If one does, it's game over!

Tacos continuously fall from the sky. IF the wizard touches them in time, they reset back to the top of the stage. IF they hit the bottom, it's game over!

The tacos leave a rainbow trail as they fall!

The wizard moves left and right with the arrow keys. He's moving so fast that he leaves an after-image of himself!

Part 1: Set up the project

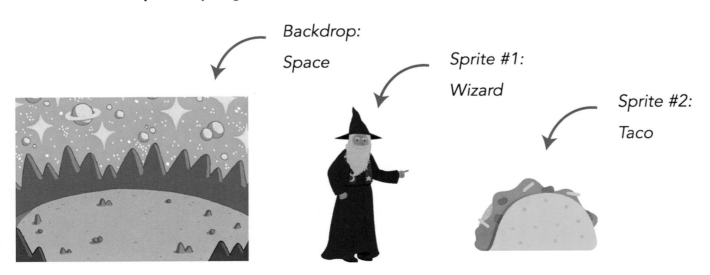

Backdrop:

Space

Sprite #1:

Wizard

Sprite #2:

Taco

Part 2: Code the Wizard

Time to get started! Make sure that you have selected your Wizard sprite and are working on its code editor. Then, start adding the code below.

1. Initialize the Wizard

Let's start by adding the code that will set the Wizard's size, where he starts on the stage, and his rotation style (how he moves left to right without flipping. Let's also tell it which of its 3 costumes to start with.

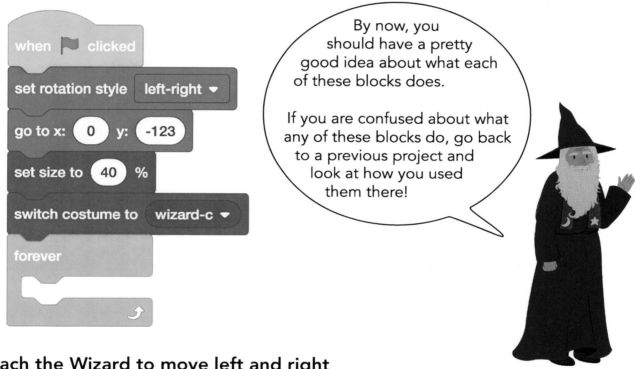

By now, you should have a pretty good idea about what each of these blocks does.

If you are confused about what any of these blocks do, go back to a previous project and look at how you used them there!

2. Teach the Wizard to move left and right

Our next step is to write code that will let our user move the Wizard to the right using the right-arrow key on our keyboard. To do so, we need our program to first check IF the right-arrow key is pressed.

1. First, bring out an if-then block.

2. Next, snap it inside of the forever loop!

Now that we have an if-then, it's time to add a condition.

Remember: a condition can either be true or false. Here, our condition will be, "Is the right-arrow key pressed?"

3. Bring out a "key (space) pressed?" block from the ⬤ Sensing tab. Then, use the dropdown arrow to select "right arrow".

4. Next, snap the "key (right arrow) pressed?" block into the diamond-shaped cut-out on the if-then block.

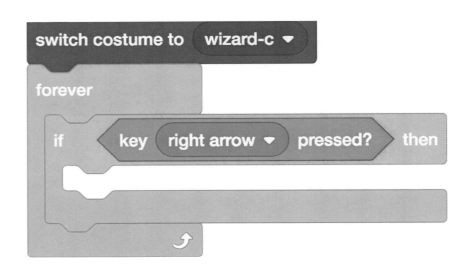

5. From the ⬤ Motion tab, bring out these two blocks and snap them inside of the if-then.

The "point in direction" block will point the wizard to the right. And the "move 3 steps" block will actually move him in that direction.

Let's now write the code to make the Wizard move to the left. We're going to use a handy trick called **Duplicating**, which allows us to easily copy any code we've already written and use it again.

6. Using your mouse, RIGHT CLICK on the if-then block that you just completed.

Or, if you are on a tablet, PRESS AND HOLD on the block for 2 seconds.

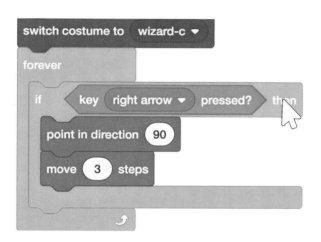

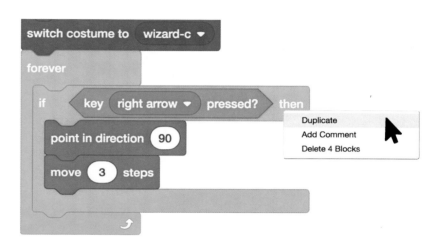

8. An exact copy of the if-then block will appear, attached to your mouse. Move your cursor with the new code blocks directly below the original if-then block...

9. ...then, place the duplicated code down by LEFT-CLICKING with your mouse.

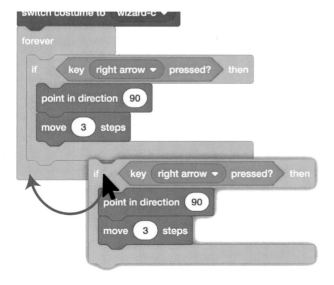

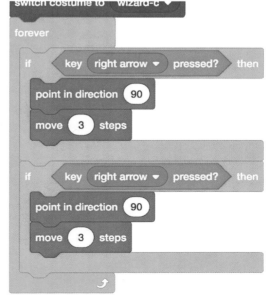

Now that we have an exact copy of our first if-then, let's make sure we edit the new code to make the Wizard move left (instead of right).

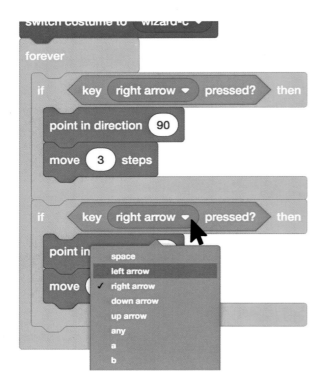

10. Click on the dropdown arrow on the second "key (right arrow) pressed?" block. Select "left arrow" from the menu.

11. Click on the dropdown arrow on the second "point in direction (90)" block. Select "-90" from the picker. This will point the Wizard to the left instead of the right.

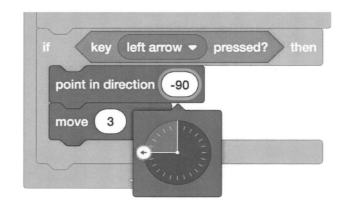

3. Test your work

Click the green flag to test your work.

- Does the Wizard move to the right when you press the right-arrow key?
- Does the Wizard move to the left when you press the left-arrow key?
- Does the Wizard stay right-side up when he moves left?

4. Create the Wizard "after-image"

We want to animate the Wizard so that it looks like he's moving super fast. The way that we will do that is by creating a slight "blur" behind the Wizard as he moves.

To do so, we will use a trick called **Cloning**.

In Scratch, we can create things called **clones** of our sprites. Clones are like temporary copies of a sprite, and they can be coded to do something completely different than the original sprite. We will use clones to "trail" behind our Wizard sprite.

1. From the ⬤ Control tab, bring out two "create clone of (myself)" blocks .

When the computer reads this block, it will create a clone of the sprite that it was placed in.

2. Place ONE "create clone of (myself) block in each if-then block, underneath the Motion blocks.

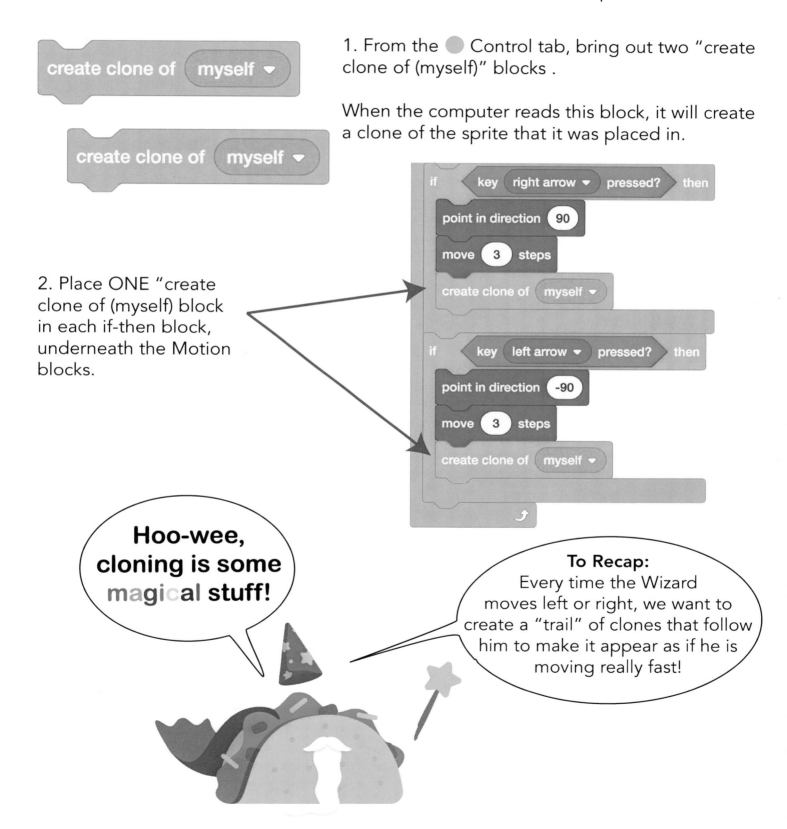

Hoo-wee, cloning is some magical stuff!

To Recap:
Every time the Wizard moves left or right, we want to create a "trail" of clones that follow him to make it appear as if he is moving really fast!

What we have just done is tell our computer program when to create a clone of the Wizard. Now, we need to write code that will tell the clone what to do once it has been created!

when I start as a clone

3. From the ⬤ Control tab, bring out a "when I start as a clone" block. This block gets triggered when a clone is created.

4. Bring out a "repeat (10)" block, and attach it to the "when I start as a clone" block.

Change the number of repeats to 20.

5. Next, bring out a "change [color] effect by 10" block from the ⬤ Looks tab, and snap it inside of the repeat loop.

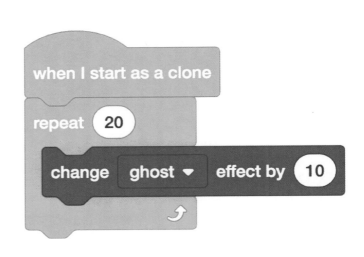

Use the dropdown arrow to select the "ghost" effect. As the ghost effect increases, the clone will get more transparent.

delete this clone

6. Finally, bring the "delete this clone" block from the ⬤ Control tab and snap it to the bottom of this code thread.

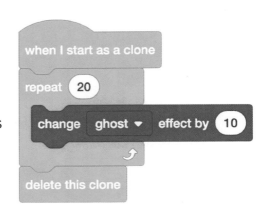

When the computer program reads this block, it will simply delete the clone that was just created. We must delete the clones, otherwise there would be too many and our computer program would crash!

5. Test your work

Click the green flag, and then try moving your Wizard left and right. Does a trail of clones appear behind him? Do they get more and more transparent as they go?

Part 3: Code the Taco

The code for the Wizard is complete! Let's now move on to coding those delicious, falling tacos. Make sure to click on the Taco sprite so that you are coding on its code editor.

The Taco must do the following things:

- It should start from a random position at the top of the stage
- It should fall down towards the bottom of the stage
- IF it touches the Wizard, THEN it should go back to the top of the stage
- IF it touches the bottom of the stage, THEN the game should end.

1. Initialize the Taco

Let's start by adding the code that will set the Taco's starting position and size.

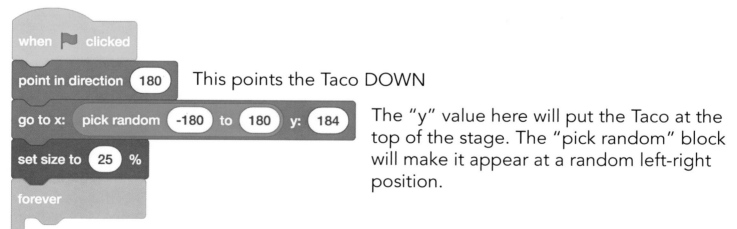

This points the Taco DOWN

The "y" value here will put the Taco at the top of the stage. The "pick random" block will make it appear at a random left-right position.

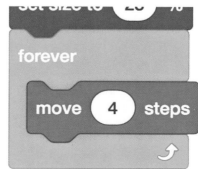

2. Next, let's get a "move (10) steps" block and put it in the forever loop. Change the 10 to a 4.

2. IF touching the Wizard...

Now, let's write the code for what should happen IF the Wizard touches the Taco. In this case, the Taco should go back to a new, random position at the top of the stage.

1. Bring out two if-then blocks, and snap them inside of the forever loop.

2. From the ● Sensing tab, bring out a "touching (mouse pointer)? block, and snap it in the condition cut-out of the first if-then block.

Use the dropdown to select "Wizard".

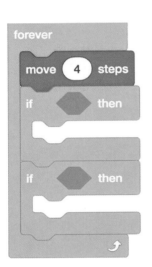

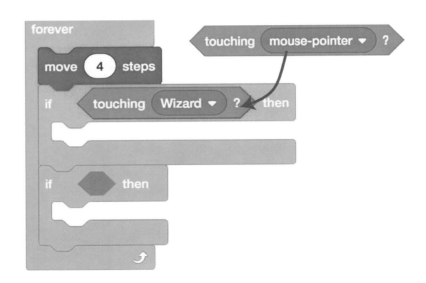

3. Bring out a "go to" block from the ● Motion tab, and snap it inside of the if-then block.

Then, from the ● Operators tab, bring out another "pick random" block and snap it inside of the "x" field. Change the numbers to (-180) to (180)

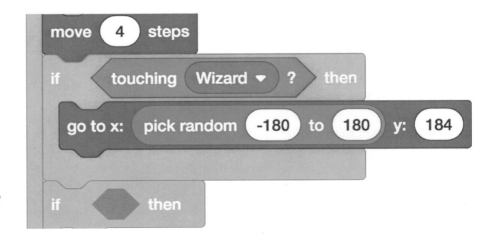

3. IF the Taco reaches the bottom of the stage...

Now, let's write the code for what should happen if the Taco hits the bottom of the stage. Basically, we want this to mean **GAME OVER**.

1. From the ● Operators tab, bring out a "less than" block. This block will compare two numbers. If the 1st number is SMALLER than the 2nd number, then the action in the if-then will happen.

Snap this block in the condition cut-out of the second if-then block. Then, type in -180 in the right side of this block.

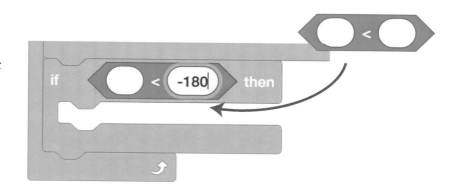

2. Next, bring out a "y position" block from the Motion tab. Snap it on the left side of the "less-than" block.

Remember that this block tracks the current up-down value of the sprite. It will let us check where the Taco is at any given moment.

3. Finally, from the ● Control tab, bring out a "stop [all]" block, and snap it inside of the if-then.

When the program reads this block, it will stop itself from running any more. It's like clicking the red stop sign next to the green flag!

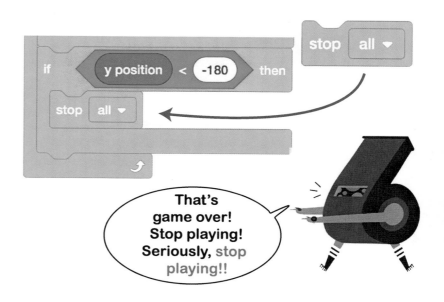

That's game over! Stop playing! Seriously, stop playing!!

4. Test your work

Let's take this baby for a test drive!

- Does the Taco start at a random position at the top of the stage?
- Does it fall towards the bottom of the stage?
- Does it go back to the top of the stage if it touches the Wizard?
- Does the game stop if it touches the bottom of the stage?

5. Rainbow Taco Trail

Now, let's wrap this project up by giving a fun visual effect to our Taco.

Remember how we gave the Wizard an "after image" using clones? Let's do the same thing for our Taco. But instead of just fading away, let's make the trail behind the Taco rainbow-colored!

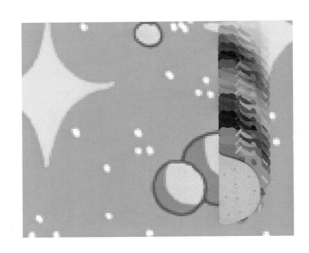

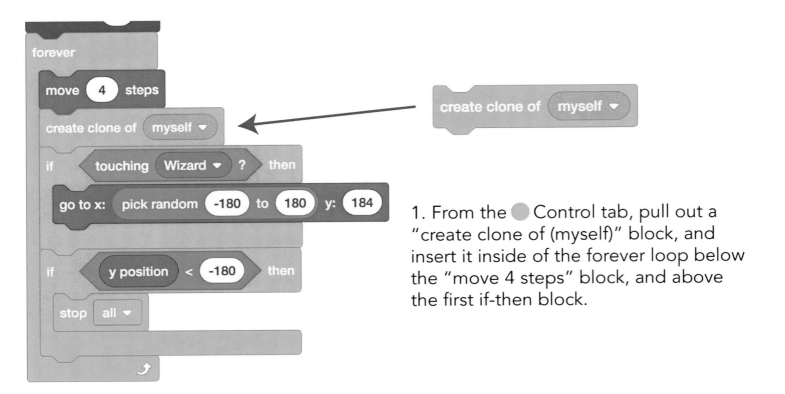

1. From the ● Control tab, pull out a "create clone of (myself)" block, and insert it inside of the forever loop below the "move 4 steps" block, and above the first if-then block.

2. Now, pull out all the blocks you see to the right into an open space on the Taco sprite's code editor.

Remember:

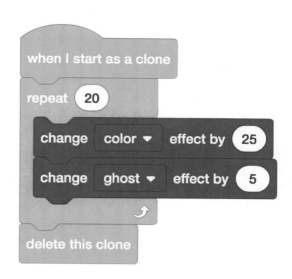

- The "when I start as a clone" block is triggered when a clone is created.
- The "repeat 20" block will repeat the code inside of itself 20 times.
- The Looks blocks will change the visual effects of the Taco clone. The "color" block will change the color of the clone, and the "ghost" block will make the clone fade away.
- The "delete this clone" block will delete the cone after it completes everything in the loop.

Part 4: Test your work

Give your program one final test. Are the Taco rainbow trails working as expected?

Part 5: Mod your work

Congrats on making your second computer game, coder! By now, you should be getting the hang of if-then statements. You also learned how to use clones and visual effects. Great work!

Save your work, then make a copy of this project to start modding.

Challenge 1: Create a second Taco sprite that falls 1 second after the first Taco sprite does (hint: RIGHT CLICK on your Taco sprite thumbnail. Then, click "duplicate").

Challenge 2: Give the Wizard a cool visual effect when he touches a Taco.

Chapter 4
Variables

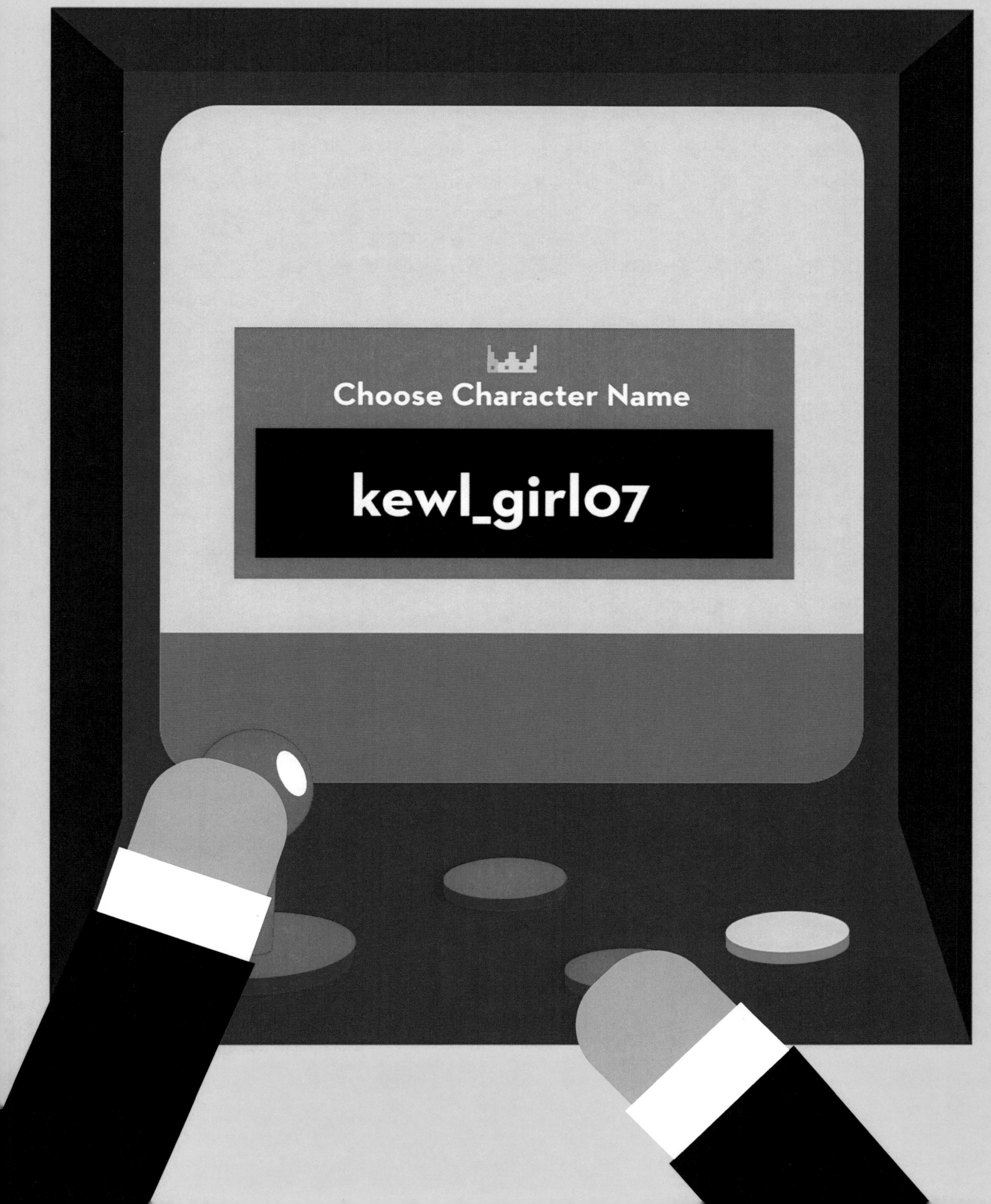
Choose Character Name
kewl_girl07

Variables

Have you ever played a game that asked you to create a username? You start a new game, and it asks you to type in a unique name to identify yourself with. So, maybe you type in something like "kewl_girl07" or "soccerdude88". After that, the game always seems to remember the name you entered, no matter how long you play for or how many times you restart the console.

But can you imagine how annoying it would be if the game *didn't* remember your name? You would have to re-enter it every time you played! And what if the game forgot your high score, or your last save? It would be chaos!

Thankfully, we can avoid awkward situations like that by teaching our programs to *remember information* using something called a **variable**.

A variable is just a box that we can put a piece of information inside of. That box is then stored inside of our program's memory, and can be accessed whenever the program needs that info.

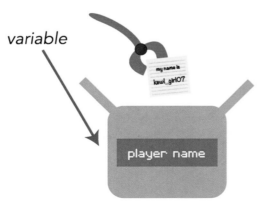

Step 1:
You or the user enters some info for the program to remember.

Step 2:
You create a variable and give it a name. The program will take the info from Step 1 and put it inside.

Step 3:
The program is asked to remember the info from Step 1, so it goes back to the variable and looks inside!

What types of info can variables store?

Variables are commonly used to store numbers and words. Here are some examples:

- Health Points (HP)

- Score

- How much time has passed

- Sprite position (x and y)

- User-entered text (like the English phrase from the Google Translate project!)

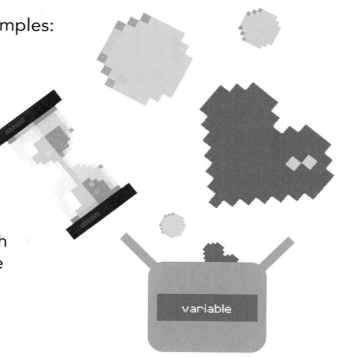

Increasing/Decreasing Variables

Even though we use variables to help our programs remember this type of information, that deosn't mean that the information will never change once it's inside of a variable.

For instance, our sprite's HP will change over time as it gets hurt or uses potions. And our Score might increase with every coin we collect.

Luckily, there are special commands/code blocks we can use to change the value inside of our variables whenever we want!

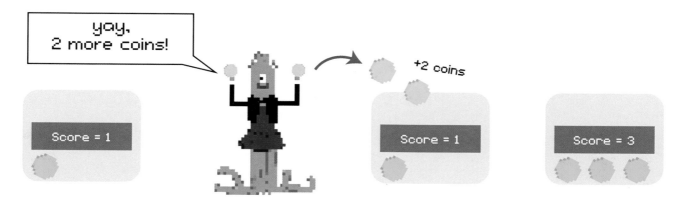

Project #6: Fish Clicker

How many fish can ya click?! That's the big question in this quick-clickin' game! Everyone knows that fish are afraid of mouse cursors (**marine biologist's note:** *this is...technically, maybe true?*) Our fish sprite will pop around the stage like a ninja, and our player will have to try to click the fish wherever it appears before it disappears again. Each time the player clicks the fish, their score will increase by 1. But they've got to go fast, because they've only got 20 seconds to click as many fish as they can!

Score (a variable) **increases** *by 1 each time you click a fish*

Timer (a variable) starts at 20 seconds, then **decreases** *by 1 each second.*

When the timer reaches 0, it's game over.

The fish appears at a random spot on the stage every second.

You have to click the fish with your mouse to score a point!

Part 1: Set up the project

Backdrop:

Underwater1

Sprite:

Fish (has 4 costumes)

Part 2: Code the Fish

Time to get started! Make sure you have your Fish sprite selected and are working in its code editor. Then, start adding the code below.

1. Teach the Fish to move to a random position, and to change costume

The Fish sprite has multiple different fish costumes. Let's build the main game loop so that the fish 1.) changes into a random fish and 2.) moves to a random position every second.

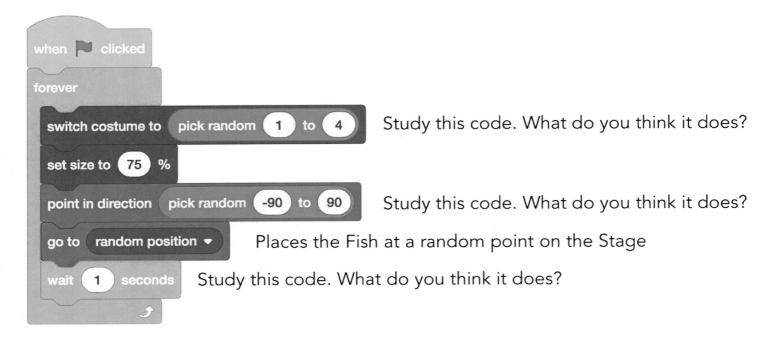

Study this code. What do you think it does?

Study this code. What do you think it does?

Places the Fish at a random point on the Stage

Study this code. What do you think it does?

2. Test your work

Click the green flag and test your work.

- Does the Fish jump to a random position on the stage?
- Does it stay there for 1 second before going to a different position?
- Does it change costume each time it moves?

Now that our Fish knows how to randomly appear and disappear, let's move on to the way that we score points: by clicking the Fish where it appears. First, we need our program to be able to keep track of how many times we click the fish.

3. Create the "score" variable

1. Click on the 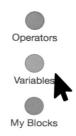 Variables tab.

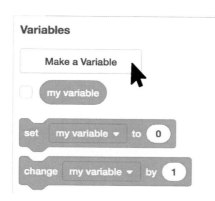

2. Click the "Make a Variable" button.

3. Your screen will turn blue, and a box will pop up in the middle. This box lets us set the variable name, along with some other options. Type in the word "score", then click "OK".

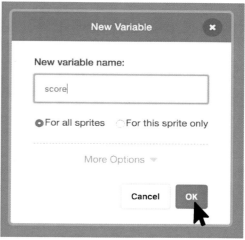

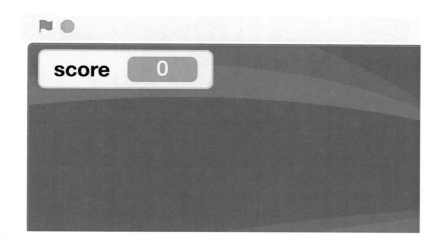

Now, take a look at your stage - the new "score" variable has appeared at the top left.

Right now, it's set to 0. Next, we'll learn how to make that number increase.

4. Set the "score" variable

Our Score variable is set to 0, but eventually it should increase as we start clickin' those Fish. But whenever we restart our game, it should reset back to 0.

1. From the ● Events tab, bring out a "when green flag clicked" block.

2. From the ● Variables tab, bring out a "set [my variable] to 0" block.

3. From the dropdown menu on this block, select "score" from the list.

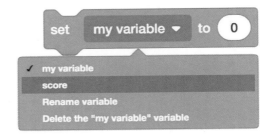

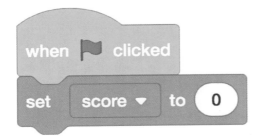
4. Next, connect these two blocks together.

5. From the ● Control tab, bring out a "forever" loop and an "if-then" block, and connect them like you see to the right.

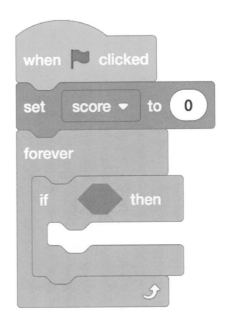

Can't touch this.

5. Increase the score when the Fish is clicked

Now, we need to teach our program *when* to increase the value in the score variable. _The program should increase the score variable value by 1 point each time the fish is being clicked by the mouse pointer._

To do this, we need the program to **check two things at the same time**: 1.) is the mouse cursor touching the Fish sprite? And 2.) Is the mouse being clicked?

Essentially, what we need to code is the following idea:

> if **fish is touching mouse AND the mouse is clicked,** then:
>   increase score by 1

1. From the ● Operators tab, bring out a "< > and <>" block.

2. Then, snap this block in the new if-then block you brought out from the last page.

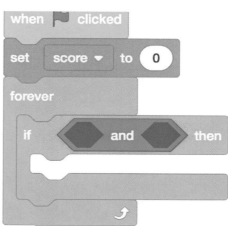

3. From the ● Sensing tab, bring out a "touching (mouse pointer)?" block.

Snap it in the left side of this new "<> and <>" block.

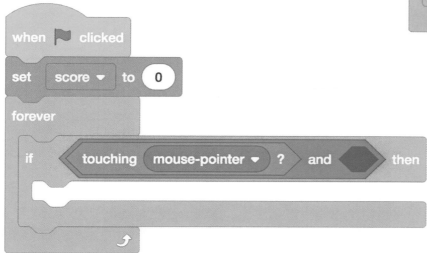

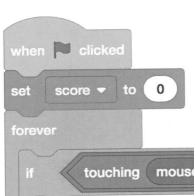

4. Again from the Sensing tab, bring out a "mouse down?" block and snap it in the right side of the "<> and <>" block.

This block checks to see if your mouse is clicked.

Synthia Tip: The "AND" block

The "AND" block is 1of 3 special blocks called Boolean (boo-lee-anne) Operators. A Boolean Operator is a type of block that lets an if-then block check for more than one condition.

For example, when the "AND" block is put onto an if-then block, that if-then block needs to look for TWO conditions to be true instead of just one. That means that BOTH conditions must be true before the action in the if-then block happens. If EITHER of htem is false, then the action can't happen.

As an example, check out our buddy, Scoop, to the left.

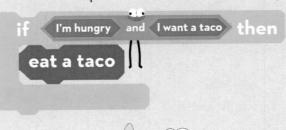

Scoop needs help deciding whether to eat a taco or not. There's two things Scoop needs to make sure are true to help it decide:

1. Is Scoop hungry?
2. Does Scoop want a taco?

In order to eat a taco, Scoop must be hungry, but it must ALSO want to eat a taco.

So, the first condition must be true, AND the second condition must be true!

Now, our code is basically asking: "Has the Fish sprite been clicked by the mouse?" IF the answer to that question becomes yes, THEN we need to increase our score by 1 point.

5. From the ● Variables tab, bring out the "change [my variable] by 1" block. Use the drop-down arrow to select the "score" variable.

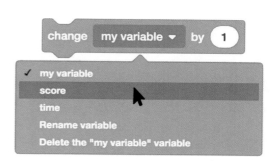

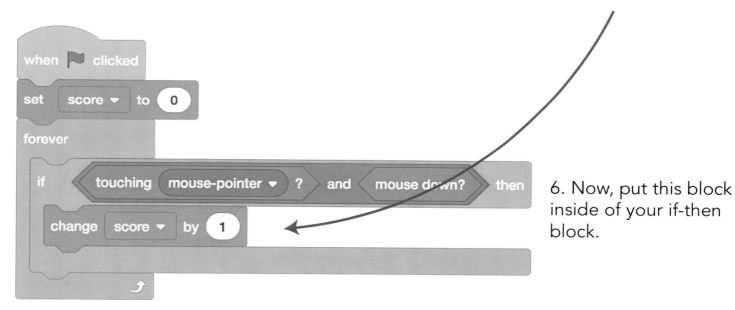

6. Now, put this block inside of your if-then block.

7. Finally, from the ● Control tab, bring out a "wait 1 seconds" block. Snap it inside of your if-then block.

Change the number in the wait block to .5

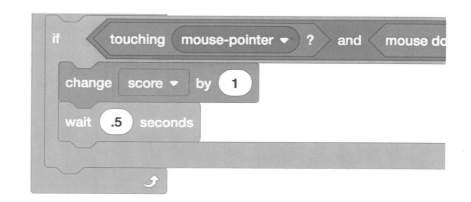

5. Test your work

Click the green flag and test your work.

- Try clicking the Fish as it appears. Does your score variable increase by 1 point each time?
- Does your score reset to 0 when you click the green flag again?

6. Create the "time" variable

Now that our program knows how to count and reset our score, it's *time* to teach our program how to count time!

For this project, we want to give the player 20 seconds to click on as many Fish as they can. When they start the game, the timer should start at 20 seconds. Then, as each second passes, the timer should count down until it hits 0 seconds. Then, the game should end!

1. Click into the ⬤ Variables tab, then click "Make a Variable".

2. The same pop-up from before will appear again. In the "New variable name:" box, type "time". Then, click "OK".

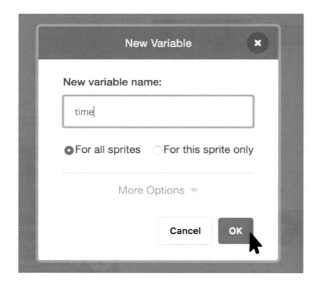

Take a look! Our new "time" variable has appeared on our stage, just below the score variable.

It's currently set to 0. Let's set it to 20 instead.

7. Set the "time" variable

1. First, bring out a "when green flag clicked" block.

2. Next, from the ● Variables tab, bring out a "set [my variable] to 0" block. Use the dropdown to select "time" from the list!

3. Connect these blocks together, then change the number in the "set [time] to 0" block to 20.

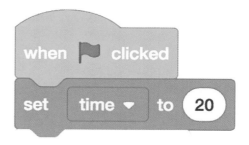

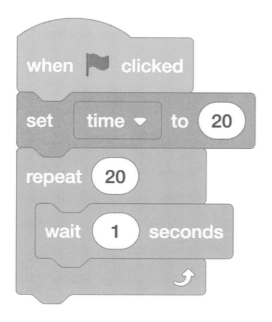

4. Now it's time to write the code that will *decrease the number* in the "time" variable by 1 each second.

From the ● Control tab, bring out a "repeat 10" loop and attach it underneath your code. Change the 10 to 20 repeats.

From the same tab, bring out a "wait 1 second" block and put it inside of the loop.

5. Bring out a "change [my variable] by 1" block. Then, use the dropdown to select "time" from the list.

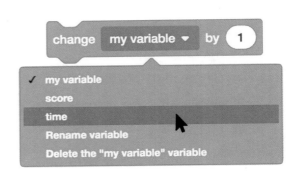

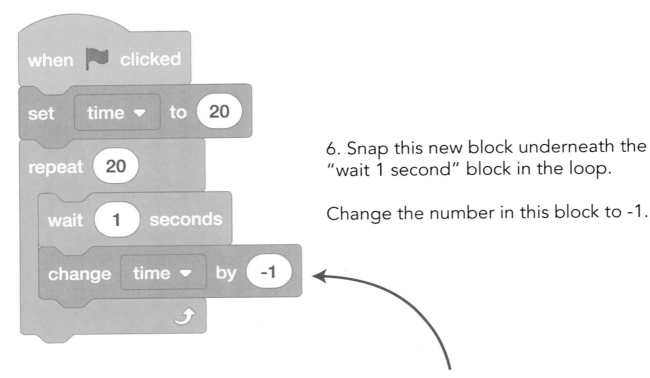

6. Snap this new block underneath the "wait 1 second" block in the loop.

Change the number in this block to -1.

This will **subtract** 1 from the number that is in the time variable. So the first time the repeat loop runs, it will:

1.) Wait 1 second
2.) Subtract 1 from 20

Now, the number stored in the time variable is equal to 19 (20 - 1 = 19). The second time the repeat loop runs, it will:

1.) Wait 1 second
2.) Subtract 1 from 19

So now, the time variable will be set to 18. Get the picture?!

8. Stop the game when time runs out

Once the repeat loop has completed all 20 repetitions, the number in the time variable will equal 0, and the game should stop.

So, from the ● Control tab, bring out a "stop [all]" block, and snap it underneath your repeat loop.

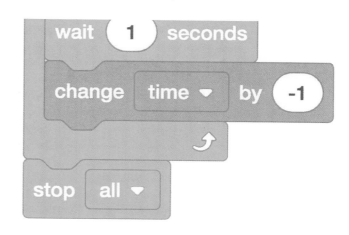

Part 3: Recap

Let's take a second to make sure we understand all of the new code we worked with in this project:

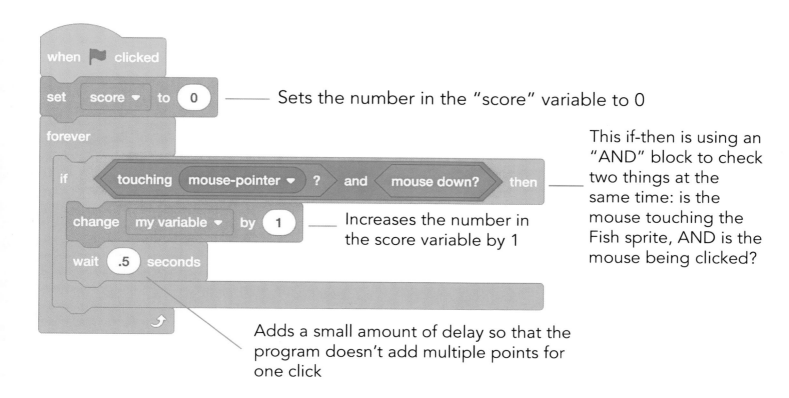

Sets the number in the "score" variable to 0

This if-then is using an "AND" block to check two things at the same time: is the mouse touching the Fish sprite, AND is the mouse being clicked?

Increases the number in the score variable by 1

Adds a small amount of delay so that the program doesn't add multiple points for one click

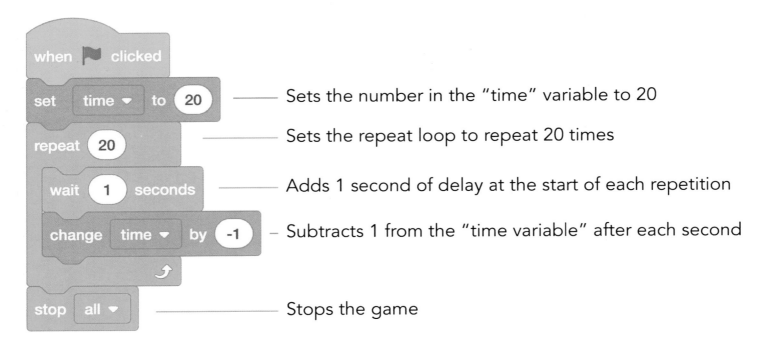

Sets the number in the "time" variable to 20

Sets the repeat loop to repeat 20 times

Adds 1 second of delay at the start of each repetition

Subtracts 1 from the "time variable" after each second

Stops the game

Part 4: Test your work

- What happens to your time variable when you start the game?
- Does it decrease by 1 each second?
- What happens when it reaches 0?
- What happens when you start the game again?

Part 5: Mod your work

Good job, coder! You've learned the last of the big four fundamental coding concepts. Save your work, then create a copy of your project and try pulling off the challenge below:

Challenge: Add a randomly appearing power-up that, when clicked, adds 5 seconds of time to your time variable. Hint: create a new sprite, and then look at the code that makes your Fish sprite appear randomly.

Project #7: Hedgehog Hedge Maze

It's common knowledge: hedgehogs love strawberries (**zoologist's note**: *this is not necessarily true*). In this exhilarating game, our player will try to navigate their way through the spiral green maze to get to the strawberry within. Here's the catch, though: the maze is spinning! And each time the player gets the hedgehog to the maze, it'll start spinning faster. And faster. And faster! Caution: this game is addicting. And SUPER frustrating. Let's get hog-wild SQUEEEEEE!

*Maze speed **increases** each time you reach the strawberry*

*Maze is constantly **spinning** - IF the hedgehog touches the maze, the hedgehog will reset back to its starting position!*

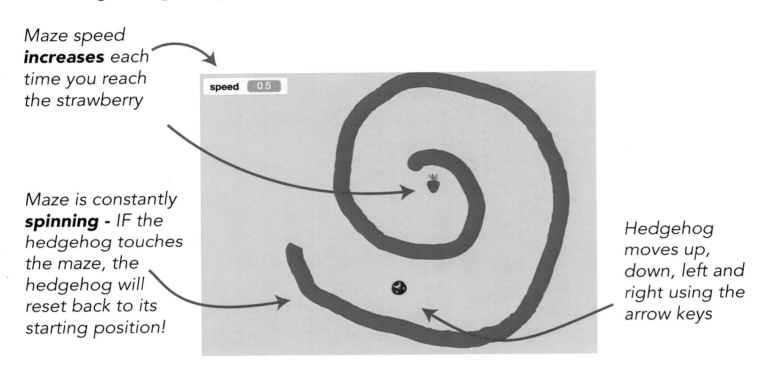

Hedgehog moves up, down, left and right using the arrow keys

Part 1: Set up the project

Backdrop:

Draw your own using the drawing tools!

Sprite:

Hedgehog

Sprite:

Strawberry

Part 2: Draw the Maze sprite

The obstacle in this game is the giant, spinning maze that separates our plucky hedgehog from the juicy strawberry. We'll need to use Scratch's drawing tools to draw this here spiral maze.

1. Create a blank sprite by hovering over the "choose a sprite" button, then selecting the paint option.

2. In the costume editor, select the paint tool from the toolbox on the left.

3. Set your fill color to a nice, dark green. Then, set your paintbrush size to 40. This will make the line that we draw nice and thick.

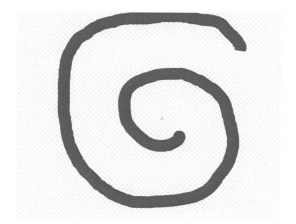

4. Finally, use your mouse to draw a nice, wide spiral. ***Make sure that the spiral is wide enough at all points for the hedgehog to move through without touching the walls*** - otherwise, your game will be impossible to beat!

Part 3: Code the Strawberry and the Maze

Each of these sprites only needs a few lines of code to work. Let's get started!

1. Code the Strawberry

Select the Strawberry sprite. Then add the following two lines of code to make the strawberry smaller. When you're done, use your mouse to move the Strawberry into the center of the stage, so that it's smack-dab in the middle of the green maze.

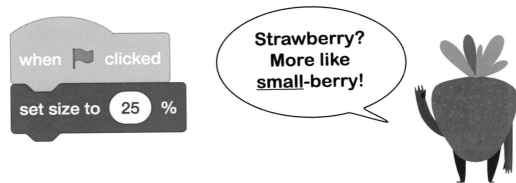

2. Code the Maze

Select your new maze sprite. Then:

1. From the ⬤ Variables tab, click the "Make a Variable" button.

In the pop-up box, name your variable "speed". Then click "OK".

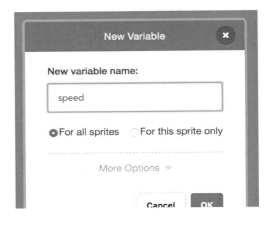

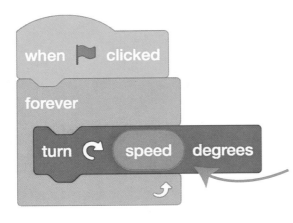

2. Bring the code you see to the left out onto your maze sprite.

From the ⬤ Variables tab, bring out the (speed) block and snap it inside of the "turn right (15) degrees" block.

The (speed) block is just a representation of our "speed" variable. Now, the maze will turn by the number inside of the speed variable (which hasn't been set - yet!)

Part 4: Code the Hedgehog

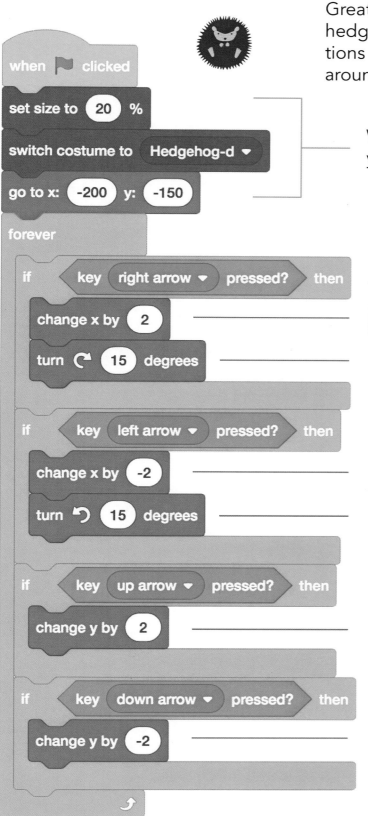

Great job. Now, it's time to start coding the hedgehog. Let's start with coding the instructions for how the hedgehog should move around the stage.

What do these three blocks do? Why do you think each of these blocks is here?

This block INCREASES the sprite's "x" position. In other words, it moves the hedgehog to the right.

This block makes the hedgehog spin to the right as it moves.

This block DECREASES the sprite's "x" position. In other words, it moves the hedgehog to the left.

This block makes the hedgehog spin to the left as it moves.

This block INCREASES the sprite's "y" position. In other words, it makes the hedgehog move up.

This block DECREASES the sprite's "y" position. In other words, it makes the hedgehog move down.

2. Set the starting speed of the maze

Our maze should start out by rotating pretty slowly. Remember that we set the speed at which the maze turns to our (speed) variable. Now, it's time to set what the speed should be at the start of the game. **We're still coding on our hedgehog sprite**, so make sure you still have it selected.

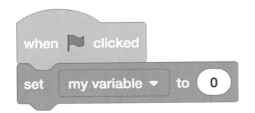

1. Bring out a "when green flag clicked" block. Then, from the ● Variables tab, bring out a "set [my variable] to 0" block.

2. Click the dropdown arrow, then select "speed" from the list.

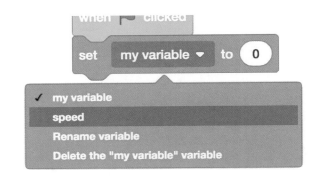

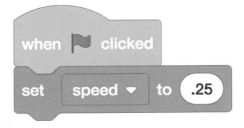

3. Set the speed variable to .25. That will make the maze turn at .25 degrees per second, which is super slow.

3. Test your work

- Can you move the hedgehog using the arrow keys?
- Does it move in the correct direction for each arrow key?
- Does the hedgehog spin when it moves left and right?
- Is the maze turning very slowly?

4. Send the Hedgehog back to its starting position

The game should get harder every time the hedgehog reaches the strawberry. To do that, we'll increase the speed that the maze is spinning IF the hedgehog touches the strawberry. The hedgehog should move back to its starting position in the bottom left-hand corner of the stage IF it touches the maze. It should also go back to the starting position IF it touches the strawberry.

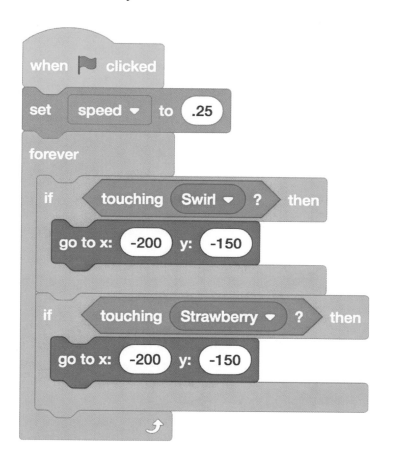

Drag out the code you see to the left:

- Forever loop

- Two if-then blocks

- Two "touching ( )?" blocks (*use the dropdown arrows on these blocks*)

- Two "go to x:(-200) y:(-150)" blocks

5. Speed the maze up

The game should get harder every time the hedgehog reaches the strawberry. To do that, we'll increase the speed that the maze is spinning IF the hedgehog touches the strawberry.

1. From the ● Variables tab, bring out the "change [my variable] to 0" block. Use the dropdown to select the "speed" variable.

Finally, set the amount that the variable should change by to .25.

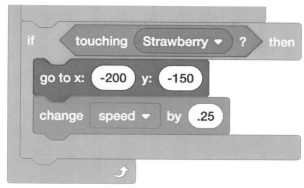

Part 5: Test your work

- Try to reach the strawberry (might be kind of hard!). What happens when you reach it?
- Does the hedgehog return to its starting position?
- Does the maze start spinning faster?

Fair warning: this game will get REALLY hard REALLY quickly. Enjoy watching your friends' and family's faces as they try and fail to get the high score!

Part 6: Mod your work

Good job! Hopefully, you're starting to get the hang of variables. Go ahead and mod your project as you see fit. Here's some difficult mods you could challenge yourself with. As always, save a copy of your work so that you always have one original, working copy!

Challenge 1: Add powerups. Make a sprite appear that, when touched, makes your hedgehog move temporarily faster, or temporarily immune to touching the maze walls.

Challenge 2: Make the maze flip the direction it spins every time the hedgehog touches it.

Challenge 3: Add some fun artistic effects to your project to make it your own!

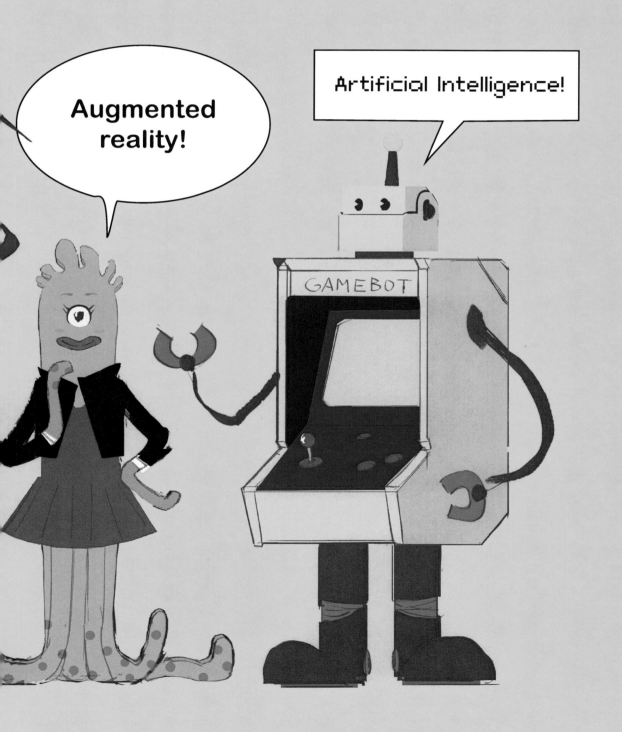

Broadcasts

Think about the "when green flag clicked" block. We use that block in basically every single project to tell our program when to start running its code.

It's an example of what's called an "event". **Computers use events to know when to do stuff.**

For example, in the comic below, the big bad boss should only appear once it receives a message calling for help from the minion. Until it does, it should just be sleeping.

In the comic above, "When I receive 'HELP!'" is an example of an event. We can create custom events just like this one in Scratch using **broadcasts**.

A broadcast has two pieces: a **caller**, and a **receiver**. For instance, the minion *calls* for help. And the big bad boss waits to *receive* the call for help before running its code. The caller can be used in one sprite's code to make another sprite do stuff.

We'll use broadcasts in our next project. See ya there!

Augmented Reality

Have you played or heard of Pokémon Go? The game came out in 2016, and hundreds of millions of people all over the world downloaded it in a matter of days. In the first few weeks after its release, people of all ages could be seen walking around outside, holding up their phones and catching Pokémon that appeared (at least on their phones) to actually be roaming around in the real world!

Pokémon Go is one of the most popular examples of a technology called **Augmented Reality (AR)**. Basically, AR overlays digital objects on top of the real world. We can hold up cameras on devices like smartphones right up in front of our faces so that we can see 1.) the real world in front of us, and 2.) digital objects that seem to magically appear in our reality.

AR apps are (as of this book's publishing) an extremely exciting and cutting edge technology. And with Scratch 3, we can create our own AR applications and games!

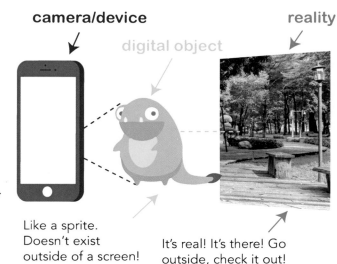

camera/device

reality

digital object

Projects the digital object onto the real-world

Like a sprite. Doesn't exist outside of a screen!

It's real! It's there! Go outside, check it out!

Project #8: Augmented Reality Fruit Slicer

Have you ever played Fruit Ninja? In that popular game, you use your finger to slice up fruit as they pop up around the screen. In this project, we're going to build our own version of that game, but way better: we're going to add Augmented Reality to ours!

For this project, you'll need a computer or tablet with a webcam or front-facing camera. The webcam will be pointed at you, *and you* (or your player) *will appear inside of the game!* As fruit flies past you, you use your hands to chop away at them.

The fruit sprites fly in from random places and glide across the entire screen

This will be you (or the person playing your game). Scratch will use your computer's webcam to track your movement.

When the camera detects you hitting the digital fruit, the fruit will explode!

Part 1: Set up your project

Sprite:

Bananas*

*Can't find the Bananas? Try adding another sprite like the apple. Then, in the Costume editor, click "Choose a Costume", then find the Bananas from the list.

Part 2: Augment reality!

Remember: augmented reality is built from two layers, 1.) the real world and 2.) the digital world. In this project, we need to see ourselves as we're playing the game so that we know where our finger is in relation to the fruit that we want to slice up.

To do this, we'll use Scratch's built-in video capture features.

1. Turn on the video

1. Click on the "Add Extension" button in the bottom left-hand corner of the editor.

2. Click on the "Video Sensing" extension to load it into your project.

Video Sensing
Sense motion with the camera.

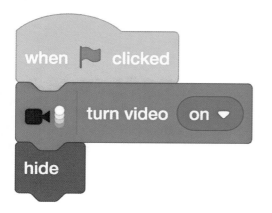

3. Bring out a "when green flag clicked" block. From the new Video Sensing tab, bring out the "turn video on" block. Then, from the ● Looks tab, bring out a "hide" block.

4. Now, click on the green flag - your computer's built-in camera should turn on, and you should now see yourself inside of the stage! Woah!!

Note: You may be asked to allow Scratch to access your camera. Make sure you grant Scratch access to do so.

2. Add your first broadcast

The code that controls how the banana sets its position and moves across the stage is going to be written under a broadcast "listener" in just a few moments. However, since we need the banana to start doing that stuff as soon as the green flag is clicked, we need to add a broadcast "caller" to run that code at the start of the game.

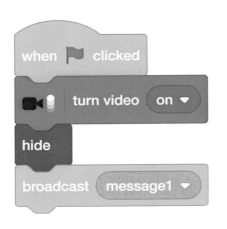

1. From the ⚪ Control tab, bring out a "broadcast (message 1)" block.

2. Use the dropdown arrow on this block to select "new message".

3. A blue pop-up box will appear that allows us to create a unique name for the broadcast. Let's call this one "reset banana". Then, click "okay".

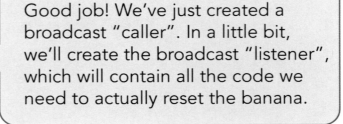

Good job! We've just created a broadcast "caller". In a little bit, we'll create the broadcast "listener", which will contain all the code we need to actually reset the banana.

3. Check if your finger hit the banana

Next, we'll write some code to see if your finger "moved across" the banana sprite fast enough to slice it apart.

1. To start, bring out a forever loop and if-then block from the ● Control tab. Then, from the ● Operators tab, bring out a "( ) > ( )" block. Snap this in the condition cut-out, then type "30" in the second box.

2. From the ● Video Sensing tab, bring out the "video motion on sprite" block. This block checks to see how fast you (or any part of you) is moving in the camera as you touch the sprite (in this case, the bananas!).

3. Next, snap this block in the left-hand side of the "( ) > (30)" block.

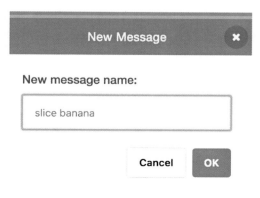

4. Finally, bring out another "broadcast (message1)" block from the ● Events tab. Place it inside of the if-then block, then use the dropdown to create a new message, "slice banana".

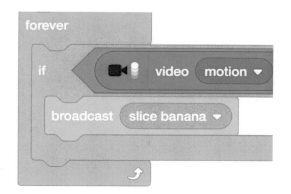

4. Reset the Banana

A few pages ago, we created a broadcast "caller" named "reset banana". Now, it's time to create the broadcast "listener". The code that gets triggered by calling this listener will make the banana move to a random corner of the screen and then fly out in a random angle. Let's get started!

1. From the ⚪ Control tab, bring out a "When I receive [reset banana]" block.

Whenever a "broadcast [reset banana" block is run by the program, the code below this block will kick in.

2. Next, bring out the following blocks and attach them to the broadcast listener.

The "wait (pick random) seconds" block is meant to add some unpredictable delay in between the banana's reappearance (unpredictable = fun!). The "set pixelate to 0" will be used to clear visual effects that we add onto the banana later. And the "show" block is meant to make sure that the banana becomes visible!

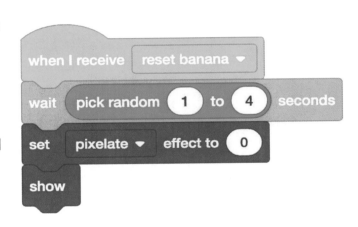

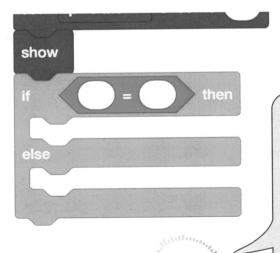

3. Now, bring out an "if-then-else" block from the ⚪ Control tab. From the ⚫ Operators tab, bring out a "( ) = ( )" block and snap it in the condition cut-out.

Synthia Tip: If-Then-Else

An "if-then-else" block lets us tell the program what to do IF the condition inside of it is false. So instead of just skipping the code it was supposed to do, we can give it something *else* to do instead!

5. Pick at random

The next step for this "reset banana" code is to randomly pick 1.) a position on the left or right side of the stage for the banana to start and 2.) a random direction for it to fly in.

To do that, we'll first have the program generate a *random* number, 1 or 2. IF the program generates a 1, then we'll have the banana start on the left side of the stage. ELSE (if its 2), then the banana will start on the right side.

1. From the ● Operators tab, bring out a "pick random 1 to 10" block, and place it in the left side of the "( ) = ( )" block. Change the "10" to a "2". On the right hand side, type the number "1".

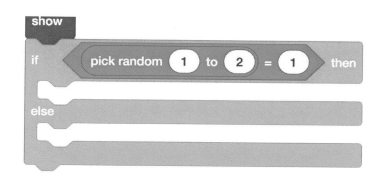

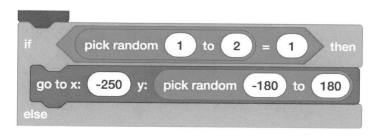

2. Using ● Motion and ● Operator blocks, recreate the code you see to the left. This will have our banana start on the left side of the screen (x: -250), and at a random up-and-down position (pick random: -180 to 180).

3. Again using ● Motion and ● Operators blocks, recreate the "glide" block you see to the right. This block will have the bananas glide to a random position on the right side of the stage, and at a random speed.

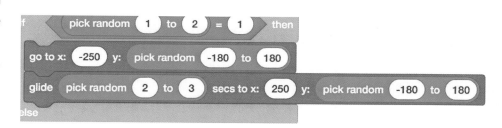

4. Finally, **copy** the code you just wrote and move the copy into the "else" portion of the "if-then-else" block. Make sure to change x positions in these blocks to "250" and "-250".

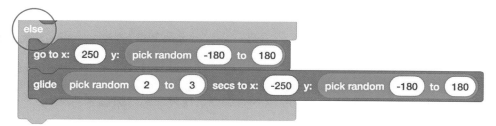

5. Finally, underneath your completed if-then-else code, add a "hide" block.

Then, add another "broadcast (reset banana)" block to the very bottom. This will make it so that after the banana reaches the other side from where it started, the whole "When I receive [reset banana]" block will repeat.

6. Create the "slicing" effect

Earlier in the project, we wrote the piece of code you see to the right.

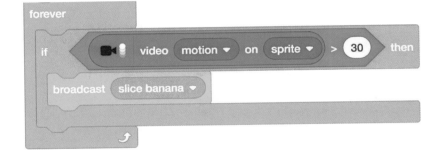

Remember: this is saying that *if* the video camera measures the speed of one of our hands moving across the banana sprite at a speed of greater than 30, *then* we will trigger the banana slicing code.

So, let's wrap up our project by writing that piece!

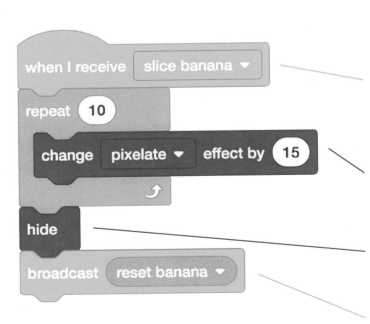

1. Bring out the code blocks and attach them in the order you see to the left.

The "When I receive [slice banana]" block is the listener for the "broadcast (slice banana) block.

The repeat block and "change pixelate" block create an effect that makes it look like the sliced fruit is fading out of existence.

The "hide" block simply hides the banana sprite once its been sliced.

Finally, the "broadcast (reset banana)" block runs all of the code under the "When I receive [reset banana]" listener.

Part 3: Test your work!

Woohoo! Good job. That was a lot of code! It's time to give our very first augmented reality project a spin.

- Does your computer webcam come on?

- Do the bananas start at a random point on the left or right side of the screen, then glide to a random point on the opposite side?

- What happens if you slice across the bananas with your hands? Does the banana "pixelate", then disappear?

Part 4: Mod your work!

Save a clean copy of your project, then try out one or all of the following ideas to modify your project:

Challenge 1: Add a sound effect from the sound effect library each time you slice the banana

Challenge 2: Add a second fruit sprite. Create new broadcasts for this new sprite, i.e. "reset apple" and "slice apple".

Project #9: Magic Tennis

In this fast-paced computer game, you'll face off against your greatest rival...the computer itself! That's right, coders: we're going to make a computer game that *plays against you.* You'll both control a wand, batting a star from one side to the other. If you miss the star and it touches your edge of the screen, then the computer scores a point! Not only that, but each time you or the computer manages to touch the star, a different magical effect will be cast, changing the look and speed of the game.

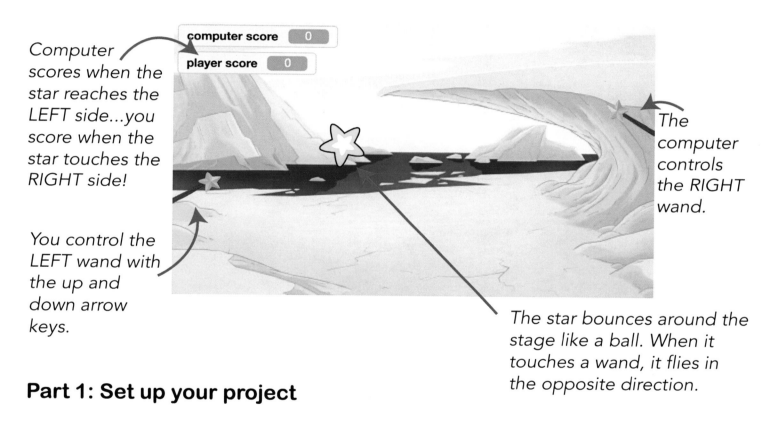

Computer scores when the star reaches the LEFT side...you score when the star touches the RIGHT side!

The computer controls the RIGHT wand.

You control the LEFT wand with the up and down arrow keys.

The star bounces around the stage like a ball. When it touches a wand, it flies in the opposite direction.

Part 1: Set up your project

Backdrop: Choose any 5!

Sprite: Wand

Sprite: Wand

Sprite: Star

Part 2: Code the Wands

Let's start this project by taking care of the code for each wand. Remember: the Wand on the LEFT will be controlled by the player (a human) using the up and down arrow keys. The Wand on the RIGHT will be controlled by the computer (an artificial intelligence).

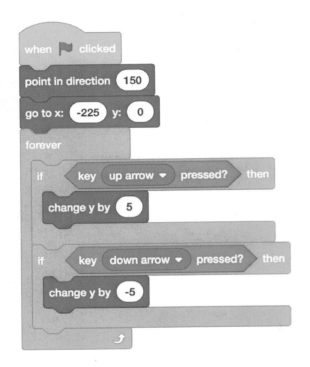

1. Code the player-controlled Wand

Select one of the Wand sprites you added to your project. Change the sprite's name to something like "Player" so that you know which wand is which.

Then, bring out all of the code you see to the left into its editor!

2. Code the computer-controlled Wand

1. Now select the other Wand sprite. Rename it "AI" or "Computer". Then, bring out all of the code you see to the right into its editor!

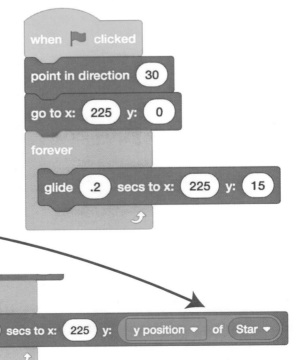

2. From the ● Sensing tab, bring out a "(x position) of (Stage)" block. Snap it into the "y" position of the glide block.

Then, use the dropdown arrows on this block to select "y position" of "Star".

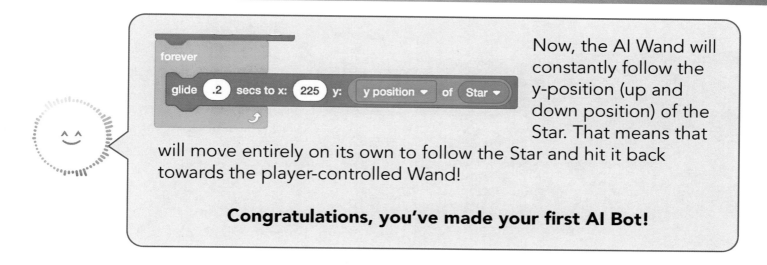

Now, the AI Wand will constantly follow the y-position (up and down position) of the Star. That means that will move entirely on its own to follow the Star and hit it back towards the player-controlled Wand!

Congratulations, you've made your first AI Bot!

3. Now, click on the green flag. Then, using your mouse, pick up and move the Star sprite to different points on the stage. Does the AI Wand move up and down as the Star does?

Part 3: Code the Star

Now that the Wands are taken care of, it's time to move onto the Star's code.

The Star should have the following features:

1.) Resets to its starting (initial) size and speed
2.) Starts in the middle of the stage, then chooses a random direction (left or right) to move
3.) Starts moving. If it touches either of the Wands, then it'll bounce in the opposite direction. If it touches an edge of the stage, it bounces off of it.
4.) When it touches a wand, a random magic spell is cast, changing something about the Star or the Backdrop!

1. Reset to initial conditions

On the Star sprite, bring out the code you see to the right. Be sure to create a variable called "speed".

Since one of the magical effects will be to slow down or speed up the Star's movement, this variable will keep track of how fast the Star should be moving.

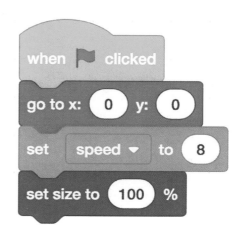

2. Pick a random direction to move

When the Star starts moving, it should pick a random direction to kick things off.

Bring out the code you see to the left and attach it to the bottom of your initialization code.

Basically, we are asking the program to pick a random number, 1 or 2. If the program randomly picks 1, then the Star will move right. ELSE, if the program randomly picks 2, it will move left.

3. Start moving, and bounce off the edges.

Next, bring out the blocks you see to the right and attach them to the bottom of the "if-then-else" block.

Be sure to take a "speed' variable block and snap it inside of the "move 10 steps" block. Now, since "speed" is set to 8, it will move 8 steps. Later, that number might increase or decrease!

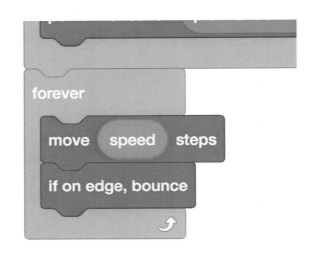

4. If touching the Player Wand, then...

Now, create a new "if-then" block and fill it with the blocks you see to the left.

First, we want there to be a small sound effect when the Star hits the Wand (*see page 35 for instructions*).

Next, the Star should change direction to a random angle facing the Computer side.

Finally, we'll create a broadcast caller called "change effect". This will trigger a random magical effect to occur later!

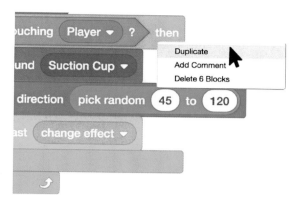

5. Duplicate!

Now that we've coded what should happen if the Star touches the Player, let's copy this code to write what should happen if the Star touches the AI.

We can reuse all of the code we just wrote. So RIGHT-CLICK (if you're using a mouse) or TAP AND HOLD (if you're using a tablet) on the if-then block, then select "Duplicate" from the menu.

5. Change the values

Snap the copied code directly below the first if-then block.

Make sure to change the "touching?" block to target the AI sprite. Finally, change the numbers in the pick random block so that the Star changes direction and points towards the Player wand.

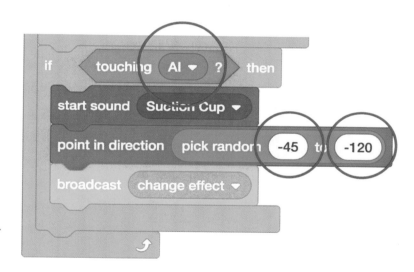

6. Test your work

- Can you move the player wand using the up and down arrow keys?

- Is the Star moving? Does it bounce on the edges of the screen? What happens when it touches your wand? The computer's wand?

- Does the computer's wand automatically follow the Star?

Part 4: Code the Magic Effects

Remember how we just created the broadcast caller, "change effect"? We'll use that caller to trigger some code that will randomly change an effect in the game. Essentially, we'll ask the program to pick a random number between 1 and 7. Then, we'll create 7 different effects that change stuff like the size, speed, and color of the Star.

That's right - this friendly game of tennis just turned into a magical duel between our two contestants!

1. Make sure you are still coding in the Star sprite. Then, from the ● Events tab, bring out a "when I receive change effect" broadcast receiver.

2. Create a new variable called "effect". Then, bring out a "set effect to 0" block and snap it under the receiver.

Then, bring out a "pick random" block and set the range to 1 to 7. Snap this block inside of the "set effect" block.

This will have the computer generate a random number, and then store it inside of the new "effect" variable.

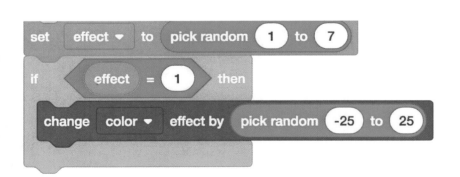

3. Now, let's create our first possible effect. Bring out the blocks you see to the left and attach them underneath the "set effect" block.

Can you figure out what this code does? It basically means that if the "effect" variable is randomly set to 1, then the color of the star should change to a random color.

4. Now, finish off the magic effects by writing the code for the next 6 possible effects.

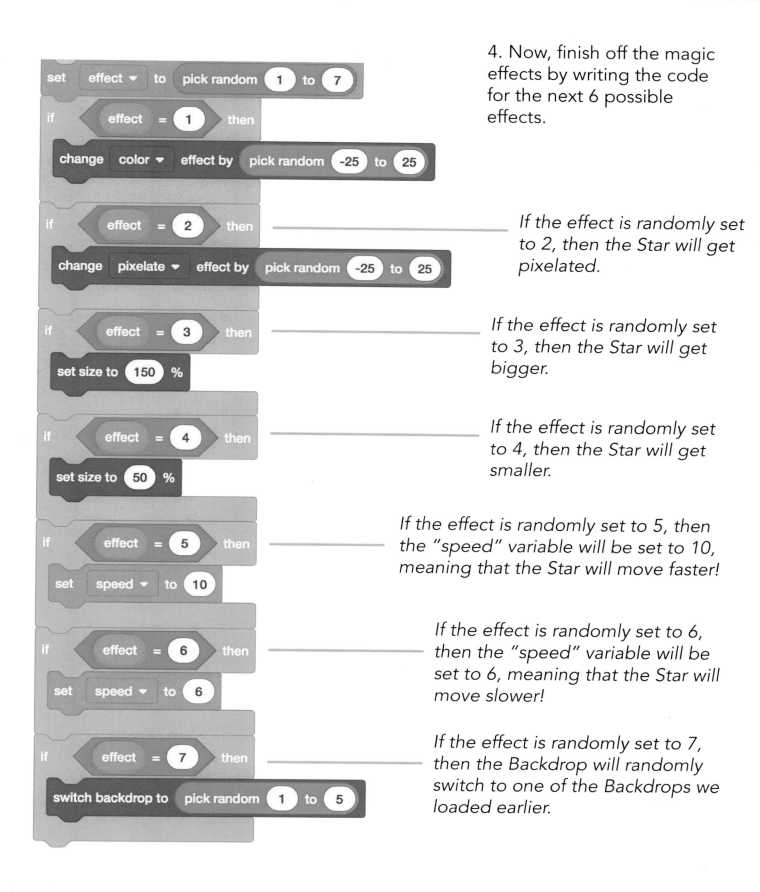

If the effect is randomly set to 2, then the Star will get pixelated.

If the effect is randomly set to 3, then the Star will get bigger.

If the effect is randomly set to 4, then the Star will get smaller.

If the effect is randomly set to 5, then the "speed" variable will be set to 10, meaning that the Star will move faster!

If the effect is randomly set to 6, then the "speed" variable will be set to 6, meaning that the Star will move slower!

If the effect is randomly set to 7, then the Backdrop will randomly switch to one of the Backdrops we loaded earlier.

Test your work

Now, click on the green flag and test your new work! What happens when you or the AI hits the Star with your wands?

Try playing for a few minutes to see if all of your effects are eventually chosen.

Part 5: Create the scoring rules

Well done, coders! Our project is nearly complete. To finish things off, we'll now write some code to control when and how the *AI* scores, and when and how the *player* scores. Let's get this show on the road!

All of this code will go in your Backdrop's code editor. So make sure to click on that and add all of the following code there.

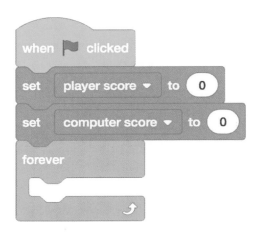

1. **Click on your Backdrop. Then, add the code you see to the left to the Backdrop's code editor.**

Make sure to create two new variables - "player score" and "computer score".

1. Code the player score

1. Now, create the following if-then block.

This if-block will check to see if the x (left-and-right) position of the Star is greater than 210. In other words, it will check to see if the Star is touching the right side of the Stage.

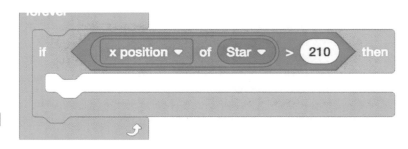

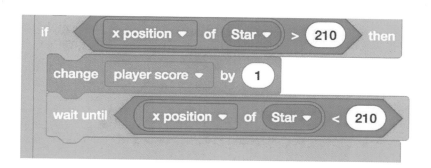

2. If the Star touches the right edge of the stage, the "player score" variable should increase by 1. The player scored a point!

The "wait until" block ensures that the player only scores 1 point at a time. Without this code, the player could score several points at once by accident.

2. Code the computer score

That wraps up the code for how the player should score. Now, let's do the same thing for the computer score.

1. The computer's score code should look almost identical to the player's score code above.

Bring out a new if-then block, and fill it with the blocks you see to the right. Make sure to stack the if-then block directly underneath the first if-then block.

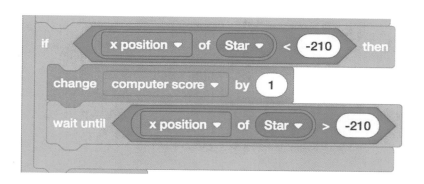

3. Decide who wins

The game should end when either the player OR the computer's score reaches 5.

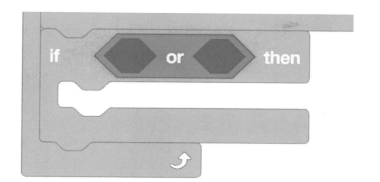

1. Bring out a new "if-then" block and snap it underneath the first two.

Then, from the ● Operators tab, bring out a "<> or <>" block. Snap it in the condition cut out.

Synthia Tip: The  **block**

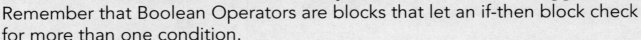

Remember the "And" block? It's one of three special blocks called **Boolean** *(boo-lee-anne)* **Operators**. Remember that Boolean Operators are blocks that let an if-then block check for more than one condition.

When an if-then block uses an "And" block, BOTH of the conditions have to be true for the code inside to run.

But with an "Or" block, only ONE of the two conditions has to be true!

For example, Tenta has been trying to eat healthy. She's set a rule for herself: IF she eats cake OR if she eats cookies, THEN she must eat a piece of broccoli.

Only one of these conditions has to be true in order for Tenta to eat a piece of broccoli. So even if she just has one lil' piece of cake and no cookies, she's still going to have to face her veggies!

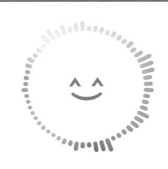

2. Now, on either side of the "<> or <>" block, drop in a "( ) > ( )" block. Then fill each of these blocks in as you see to the right.

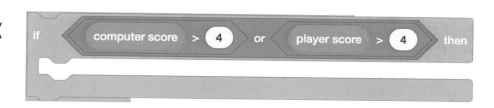

4. Make your project speak!

Scratch 3 allows us to add text-to-speech functionality to our projects. That means that our projects can now talk out loud! Let's announce "Game Over" to our players at the end of the game.

1. Click on the "add extension" button. Then, click on the "Text to Speech" button.

2. Now, click on the new 🔊 "Text to Speech" tab in the code palette.

Find the "speak (Hello!)" block, and snap it inside of your new if-then block. Change the text to "Game Over!"

3. Last step, coders! From the Control tab, bring out a "stop all" block. Snap it inside of the if-then, underneath the new "speak" block.

Part 6: Test your work!

Great job, coders! Give your project one final test to make sure everything's working as expected.

- Can you move the player wand with the up and down arrows?

- Does the AI wand move on its own?

- Does the Star bounce around the stage? What happens if it touches one of the wands?

- What happens if the Star touches the right side of the stage? Which score increases?

- What happens if the Star touches the left side of the stage? Which score increases?

- What happens when one player reaches a score of 5 (make sure to turn your speakers up!)?

Part 7: Mod your work!

Save a clean copy of your project, then try out one or all of the following ideas to modify your project:

Challenge 1: Add more magical effects to your project!

Challenge 2: Add an option before the game starts to disable the AI and let a second human play against you instead.

Artificial Intelligence:
Machine Learning

One of the most powerful uses of computer programming is the creation of artificial intelligence (commonly referred to as AI). Engineers who specialize in AI try to make machines that think and act like humans.

For example, have you ever thought about how humans learn stuff? One of our most powerful abilities as human beings is to learn from our experiences and create patterns out of the things we observe.

Some programmers specialize in a field called **Machine Learning**, which focuses on creating programs that try to learn in the same way that humans do.

At the time of this writing, we (as humans) are still a looooong ways away from creating a machine that is truly as smart as a human being. However, we can create our own basic version of a learning machine in Scratch 3!

Project #10: AI ChatBot

Get ready to make a new virtual intelligence! In this project, we're going to make our very own ChatBot application that slowly learns how to have a conversation with you. Throughout this project, you'll teach your new ChatBot how to respond to phrases.

Then, when you're ready, you can share this project and have people all over the world help your new ChatBot learn all sorts of phrases.

The more more conversations your ChatBot has, the smarter it will get!

The ChatBot remembers conversations it has had before. If it recognizes something the user says, it will give the response it already knows.

The user interacts with the ChatBot by typing messages to it. The Bot will remember everything the user says to it!

Part 1: Set up the project

Backdrop:
Room 1

Sprite:
Devin

Part 2: Code the main application loop

Our "main application loop" will basically decide whether the ChatBot should **respond** with something it already knows how to say, or **learn** something new.

1. Set the starting conditions

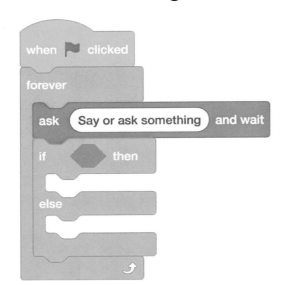

1. Bring out the blocks you see to the left and attach them in this order. Make sure to change the text in the "ask" block!

2. Create a list!

In the last step, we used an "ask" block to ask our user to say something to our AI. Now, our AI is going to need to start remembering everything that users are telling it. To do this, we're going to create something called a **list**.

A **list** is like a variable, except instead of just storing ONE thing, a list stores an UNLIMITED number of things. We can add, remove, or use entries into our list at any time. Let's get started creating our first list!

1. From the ⬤ Variables tab, click on the button that says, "Make a List"

Make a List

2. A blue dialog box will appear asking you to name your new list.

We're going to name this one "prompts", since it will store things that our user will say to or ask our AI.

3. Nice job! Now, you'll see that a bunch of new red blocks have appeared in our ⬤ Variables tab. These blocks allow us to do stuff to our new "prompts" list, like adding or removing or grabbing entries from our list.

Let's go ahead and take out the "prompts contains (thing)?" block.

This block checks to see if some item, "thing", *exists* in our prompts list or not.

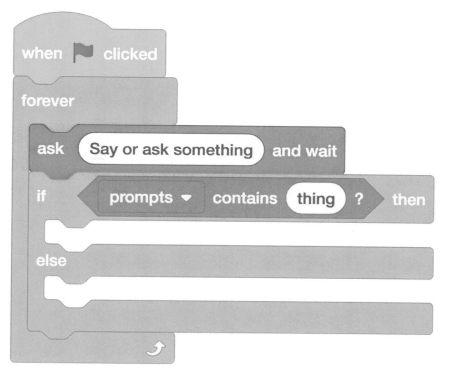

4. Now, go ahead and snap this block in the condition cut-out of the if-then-else block.

We are going to check if the "prompts" list contains the answer to the "ask" block above!

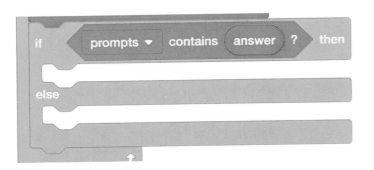

5. From the ⬤ Sensing tab, bring out an "answer" block and snap it in the "prompts" block.

3. Create the broadcast callers

There are only two things that the AI can do: respond with something it already knows how to say, or learn something new.

After the AI decides whether the thing that the user just said exists in the "prompts" list, **it will trigger one of two broadcasts**.

1. From the ⬤ Events tab, bring out a "broadcast (message) and wait" block.

Snap this in the "if" portion of the if-then-else block. Then, use the dropdown to create a new message, "respond".

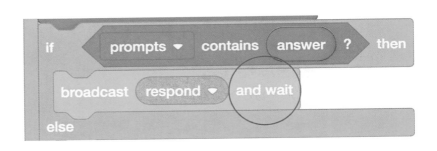

"Broadcast" vs. "Broadcast and wait"

Normally, when we use a "broadcast (message)" block to call a broadcast listener, we are telling the broadcast listener to run its code at the same time as any other code that's still running.

A "broadcast and wait" block, however, forces **the script that called it** to pause **until all of the listener code has completed**.

Confused? Don't worry! We'll explore this more in just a second.

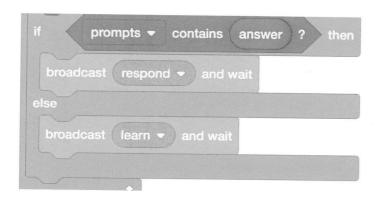

2. Next, bring out another "broadcast (message) and wait" block and snap it in the "else" portion of the if-then-else block.

Change this message to "learn".

Part 3: Teach the AI to LEARN!

If the AI has never heard someone say what the user just said before, it has to:

1.) Add what the user said to its memory (the "prompts" list)
2.) Ask the user how to respond to that statement in the future

This way, the AI actually learns and remembers what the user said and how to respond to it in case anyone else ever asks them the same thing.

1. From the ⚪ Events tab, bring out a "when I receive (learn)" block.

2. From the ⚫ Variables tab, bring out an "add (thing) to prompts" block.

This block adds anything in the text field to the "prompts" list!

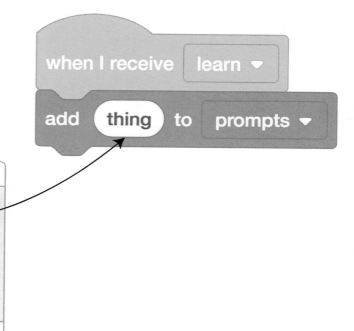

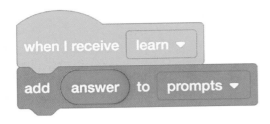

3. From the ⬤ Sensing tab, bring out an "answer" block and snap it in the "add (thing) to prompts" block.

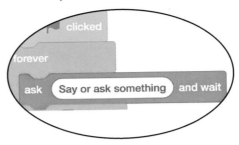

This "answer" block is coming from the "ask" block we added in the first step.

2. Learn how to respond to the new prompt

The new prompt has been added to the "prompts" list. So now it's time to learn how to respond to that prompt in the future.

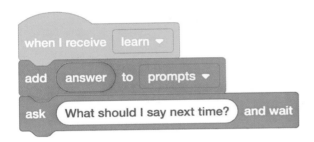

1. Bring out a new "ask" block from the ⬤ Sensing tab.

Change the text to something like *"Sorry, I don't know how to respond to that yet! What should I say next time?"*

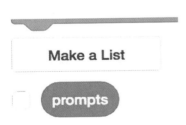

2. Next, we need to create a new list that will remember all of the responses that the AI knows.

From the ⬤ Variables tab, click "Make a List" again.

Then, in the dialog box, name this new one "responses"

New List

New list name:

responses

⬤ For all sprites   ⬤ For this sp[

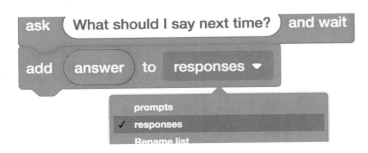

3. Now, bring out another "add (thing) to prompts" block. Snap it below all of your code.

Use the dropdown arrow on this block to select the "responses" list.

Finally, bring out another "answer" block and snap it in this "add (thing) to responses" block.

Recap!

Remember: *the code triggered by the "learn" broadcast is called when the AI doesn't recognize the user's phrase.*

In the last few pages, we added code that will allow the AI to add the new phrase to its memory bank. It also allows it to learn how to respond to that phrase in the future.

For example, here's how the first conversation with our user might go:

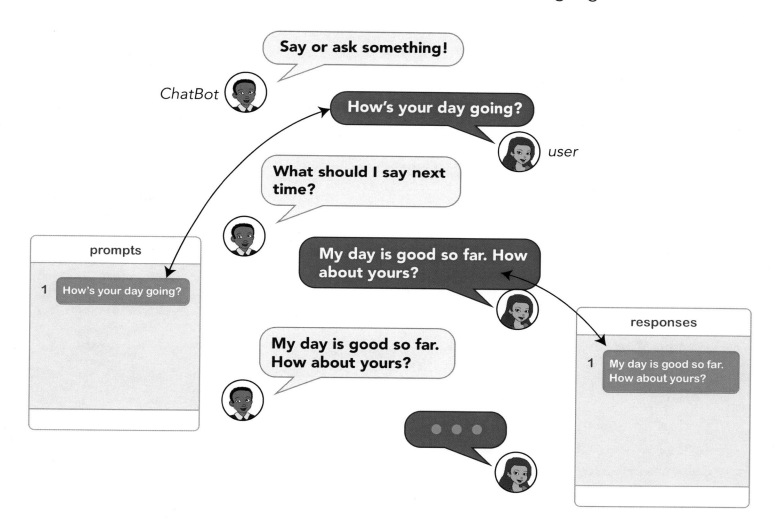

See how the first part of the conversation - "How's your day going?" - is added to the prompts list? And how the response that the user suggests - "My day is good so far. How about yours?" - is added to the "responses" list?

In the next few pages, we'll learn how to make this happen in our project.

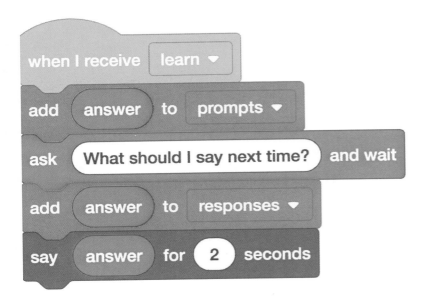

4. Finally, we want our AI to say the response it was just taught so the user knows the AI learned it.

From the ● Looks tab, bring out a "say (Hello!) for 2 seconds" block.

Snap in another "answer" block where it says "Hello!"

Test your work

- Does the AI prompt you to say something?
- Does it ask you what it should say the next time someone says that to them?

Synthia Tip: Hiding and resetting lists

You might notice that your two lists are starting to crowd your stage. To hide the lists, simply click on the checkboxes next to each list in the Data tab.

If you ever want to DELETE the contents of both lists, simply write and then click on the following code. **But, don't forget to delete this code immediately afterwards, otherwise your AI will never remember anything!**

Part 4: Help the AI learn to recognize when it knows something

In the previous steps, we taught the AI how to learn prompts (things that a human would say to the AI), and responses to those prompts. The prompts are stored in one list, and the responses are stored in a separate list.

For example, the contents of our lists might now look something like this:

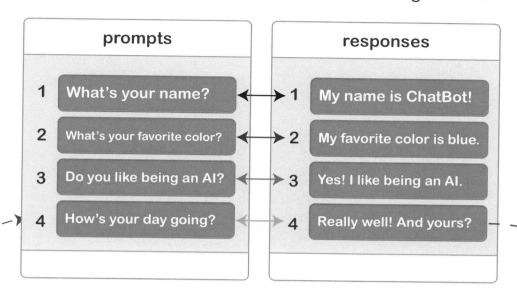

prompts			responses	
1	What's your name?	↔	1	My name is ChatBot!
2	What's your favorite color?	↔	2	My favorite color is blue.
3	Do you like being an AI?	↔	3	Yes! I like being an AI.
4	How's your day going?	↔	4	Really well! And yours?

Notice how each prompt has a matching response? And that each pair has the same number?

Now that we've taught our AI some prompts and responses, we need to teach it to recognize when someone types in a prompt that it already knows. And when it does, it needs to find the correct response to that prompt. For example:

NOTE: Grammar and spelling are important! Our AI will only recognize phrases that exactly match what's stored in its memory.

1. Find the correct response

1. From the ⬤ Events tab, bring out a "when I receive (respond) block.

2. Next, from the ● Variables tab, create a new variable and name it "response". Snap a "set [response] to 0" block to the "when I receive (respond)" block.

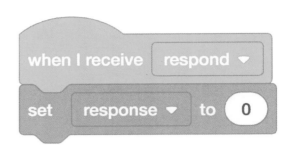

3. Again from the ● Variables tab, bring out an "item # of (thing) in prompts" block. Snap it in the "set (response) to 0" block.

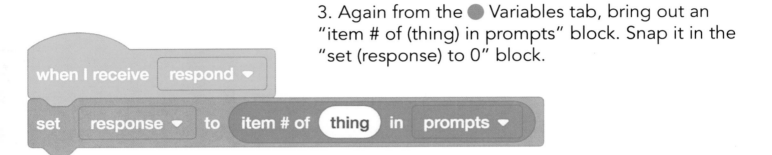

4. Next, bring out an "answer" block and snap it in the "item # of (thing) in prompts"

What does this code mean?

Remember that every item in a list is numbered. Also remember that we're trying to find the correct response to a known prompt, meaning that _the response is in the same position (has the same number) as its matching prompt_!

So basically, this code is saying "Take the number of the known response in the prompts list, and put that number inside of a variable called 'response'."

3. Find and say the correct response

Now that we know where the prompt is in the prompt list (what its number is), we can use it to find the correct response from the response list. Let's give it a shot!

1. Bring out the "say" block from the ● Looks tab. Snap it underneath the "response" variable block. Change the 2 to a 4.

2. From the Variables tab, bring out a red "item (1) of prompts" block and snap it into the "say (Hello!) for (4) seconds" block.

Next, click on the dropdown arrow on this block to select the "responses" list.

3. Finally, from the ● Variables tab, bring out a "response" block. Snap it in the "item (1) of responses" block.

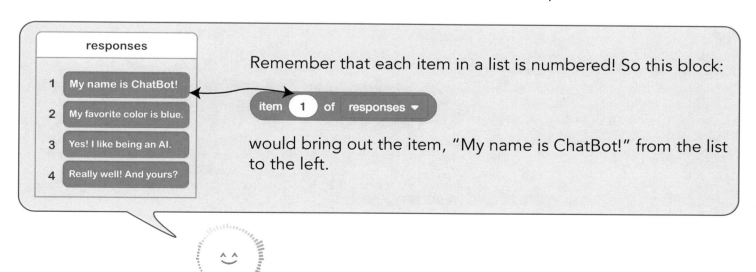

Remember that each item in a list is numbered! So this block:

would bring out the item, "My name is ChatBot!" from the list to the left.

Recap!

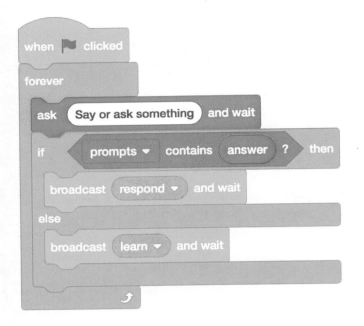

This is the main application loop. It starts by asking the user to say or ask something to the AI.

Then, it checks to see if what the user just said is an item in the "prompts" list.

It uses "broadcast ( ) and wait" blocks to trigger the correct code in either case.

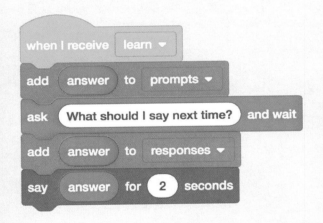

Triggered IF the AI doesn't recognize the phrase from the "ask" block in the main application loop.

First, it takes the phrase and stores it as a new prompt in the "prompts" list. Then, it uses a new ask block to ask the user for a suggestion on how to respond to that exact phrase in the future.

The AI takes that suggested response, and stores it in a list called "responses".

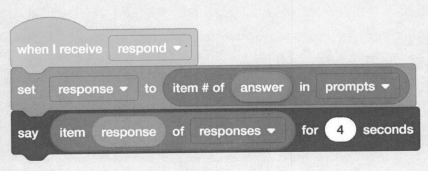

Triggered IF the AI *does* recognize the phrase from the "ask" block in the main application loop.

First, it finds the position (number) of the recognized phrase in the prompts list. It stores that number in a variable called "response".

Next, it uses the "response" variable to find the matching response in the "responses" list.

Part 4: Test your work!

Coders, that was some complicated code! Go back over this project build a few times and make sure you understand what our code does.

Then, when you're ready, click the green flag and test your program out.

- When you say something the AI doesn't recognize, does it ask you to suggest a response it should use in the future? Then, does it say that response back to you?

- Try saying something you've already said to the AI before. Does it say the response you suggested it to use?

- Turn on your list views to see all of the prompts and responses that have been added so far. Do they all match up? If there's an error or mismatch somewhere, try resetting the list and try again.

Part 5: Mod your work!

Save a clean copy of your project, then try to do the suggested mod below. Heads up, coder: **this is a very difficult mod**. Don't be afraid to find help from the Scratch community or people you know who know how to code!

Challenge 1: Figure out how to make your Chatbot recognize prompts that are similar to prompts it already knows, even if the grammar is different. For example, if your Chatbot already knows,"**What's your favorite color?**", then it should recognize that someone saying "**whats your favorite color**" is essentially the same thing.

Congratulations!

Well done, coder! You've made it to the end of the book. And (*if you didn't just skip ahead to see what the last page looks like!*) that means that you've completed 10 incredible coding projects with Scratch 3. That's a huge accomplishment - you should feel really good about that!

What's next?

Now that you've finished this book, it's time to get out there and start creating projects, apps, and games of your own design. You know more than enough about the fundamentals of coding to start bringing your own ideas to life. And that's where the real fun begins!

Want to keep learning? Visit us at www.codecampus.com to find online courses about everything from developing websites with HTML and CSS to designing your own graphics with Photoshop!

Talk to us!

We'd love to hear from you. With your parents' permission, show us the projects you code on Scratch 3! Tweet at us (@codeCampusED), or find us on Scratch (@codecampus).

Bye for now!

Made in United States
North Haven, CT
16 January 2023

31143642R00084